MathFlare

Name: _______________________

Class: __________

Teacher: _______________________

Introduction

As parents and educators, we recognize the pivotal role mathematics plays in shaping a child's academic journey and future success. Yet, the path to mathematical proficiency can often seem daunting, fraught with challenges and complexities. That's where the transformative power of MathFlare Workbooks shine through, illuminating the way forward with clarity, precision, and purpose.

Introducing MathFlare Workbooks – a beacon of guidance, a testament to excellence, and a catalyst for achievement. Crafted with meticulous care and expertise, MathFlare Workbooks stand as paragons of educational excellence, designed to nurture young minds, ignite a passion for learning, and develop a deep-rooted understanding of mathematical concepts.

Picture this: your child eagerly delves into the pages of Mathflare Workbook, greeted by a step-by-step guide illuminated with vivid examples that demystify complex mathematical concepts. With each turn of the page, they embark on a journey of discovery, encountering thoughtfully curated practice questions that reinforce learning and hone problem-solving skills. And when they unveil the answers to those very questions, a sense of accomplishment blossoms within them – a tangible reward for their hard work and dedication.

But MathFlare Workbooks are more than just tools for learning; they are pathways to comprehension, fostering a deep-seated understanding of mathematical concepts through a sequential, logical flow. From fundamental principles to advanced problem-solving strategies, every chapter builds upon the last, ensuring a robust foundation upon which future knowledge can be constructed.

As parents, we yearn for nothing more than to see our children thrive, to witness the spark of inspiration ignited within them as they conquer academic challenges with confidence and poise. MathFlare Workbooks serve as partners in this noble endeavor, offering not just practice questions, but the keys to unlocking a world of opportunity.

And for teachers, MathFlare Workbooks stand as invaluable allies in the quest to cultivate mathematical proficiency in the classroom. With answers readily available, instructors can focus on guiding and nurturing their students, confident in the knowledge that MathFlare Workbooks provide a solid framework upon which to build.

In the pages of MathFlare Workbooks, we find not just the promise of academic excellence, but the seeds of a brighter tomorrow. So let us embrace the power of mathematics, let us champion the journey of learning, and let us pave the way for a generation of young minds poised to shape the world. With MathFlare Workbooks as our guide, the possibilities are infinite, and the future, bright.

Table of Contents

MathFlare
MATH
WORKBOOK
Grade 2
Step by Step Guide
and Essential Practice
with Answers
Addition
Subtraction
Multiplication
Place Value and
Expanded Notations
Geometry
MathFlare Publishing

MathFlare
MATH
WORKBOOK
Grade 2-3
Step by Step Guide
and Essential Practice
with Answers
Addition
Subtraction
Multiplication
and Division
Place Value and
Expanded
Notations
Geometry
MathFlare Publishing

MathFlare
MATH
WORKBOOK
Grade 3
Step by Step Guide
and Essential Practice
with Answers
Multiplication
and Division
Decimals
Place Value and
Expanded
Notations
Fractions
and Geometry
MathFlare Publishing

MathFlare
MATH
WORKBOOK
Grade 1
Step by Step Guide
and Essential Practice
with Answers
Counting and
Numbers
Addition and
Subtraction
Place Value and
Expanded
Notations
Understanding
Time
MathFlare Publishing

MathFlare
MATH
WORKBOOK
Grade 1-2
Step by Step Guide
and Essential Practice
with Answers
Counting and
Numbers
Addition and
Subtraction
Place Value and
Expanded
Notations
Understanding
Time
MathFlare Publishing

MathFlare
MATH
WORKBOOK
Grade 3-4
Step by Step Guide
and Essential Practice
with Answers
Addition
Subtraction
Multiplication
Division
Place Value and
Expanded
Notations
Fractions
and Geometry
MathFlare Publishing

MathFlare
MATH
WORKBOOK
Grade 4
Step by Step Guide
and Essential Practice
with Answers
Addition
Subtraction
Multiplication
Division
Place Value and
Expanded
Notations
Fractions
and Geometry
MathFlare Publishing

MathFlare
MATH
WORKBOOK
Grade 4-5
Step by Step Guide
and Essential Practice
with Answers
Multiplication
Division
Place Value and
Expanded
Notations
Fractions
and Geometry
Unit
Conversion
MathFlare Publishing

MathFlare
Grade 5
MATH WORKBOOK
Step by Step Guide and Essential Practice with Answers
Multiplication Division
Place Value and Expanded Notations
Fractions and Geometry
Unit Conversion
MathFlare Publishing

MathFlare
Grade 5-6
MATH WORKBOOK
Step by Step Guide and Essential Practice with Answers
Multiplication Division
Place Value and Expanded Notations
Fractions and Geometry
Units and Statistics
MathFlare Publishing

MathFlare
Grade 6
MATH WORKBOOK
Step by Step Guide and Essential Practice with Answers
Integers and Statistics
Arithmetic and Pre-Algebra
Fractions and Geometry
Ratio and Percentage
MathFlare Publishing

MathFlare
Grade 6-7
MATH WORKBOOK
Step by Step Guide and Essential Practice with Answers
Arithmetic and Pre-Algebra
Ratio, Percent Proportion
Geometry
Statistics
MathFlare Publishing

MathFlare
Grade 7
MATH WORKBOOK
Step by Step Guide and Essential Practice with Answers
Pre-Algebra
Ratio, Percent Proportion
Geometry
Statistics
MathFlare Publishing

MathFlare
Grade 7-8
MATH WORKBOOK
Step by Step Guide and Essential Practice with Answers
Pre-Algebra
Ratio, Percent Proportion
Geometry and Cartesian Plane
Statistics
MathFlare Publishing

MathFlare
Grade 8-9
MATH WORKBOOK
Step by Step Guide and Essential Practice with Answers
Pre-Algebra
Ratio, Proportion and Percentage
Linear Equations
Geometry and Cartesian Plane
MathFlare Publishing

MathFlare
Grade 8
MATH WORKBOOK
Step by Step Guide and Essential Practice with Answers
Pre-Algebra
Percentage
Linear Equations
Geometry
MathFlare Publishing

Solving Two-Step Equations

Solving two-step equations involves finding the value of the variable that makes the equation true. In a two-step equation, two operations (addition, subtraction, multiplication, or division) are performed on the variable.

The goal is to isolate the variable on one side of the equation by performing inverse operations in the reverse order of operations.

For example:

Given the equation $18 = (10 + b) - 2$, where we want to solve for b.

To solve for b, we need to undo the operations that have been performed on b.

1. Undo the subtraction by adding 2 to both sides:

$$18 + 2 = (10 + b) - 2 + 2$$

$$20 = 10 + b$$

2. Undo the addition by subtracting 10 from both sides:

$$20 - 10 = 10 + b - 10$$

$$10 = b$$

So, the solution to the equation is $b = 10$

Let's substitute $b = 10$ back into the original equation to verify if it satisfies the equation:

Original equation:

$$18 = (10 + b) - 2:$$

Substitute b = 10:

$$18 = (10 + 10) - 2$$

simplify:

$$18 = 20 - 2$$

$$18 = 18$$

Since the equation simplifies to 18 =1 8, it confirms that our solution b = 10 is correct.

Solving Multi-Step Equations

Solving multi-step equations involves finding the value of the variable that makes the equation true. In a multi-step equation, multiple operations (addition, subtraction, multiplication, or division) are performed on the variable.

The goal is to isolate the variable on one side of the equation by performing inverse operations in the reverse order of operations.

Example:

Given the equation $-3m - m = -8$, where we want to solve for m.

To solve for m, we need to undo the operations that have been performed on m.

1. Combine like terms on the left side:

$$-3m - m = -4m$$

2. Substitute the combined term back into the equation:

$$-4m = -8$$

3. Undo the multiplication by dividing both sides by $-4-4$:

$$\frac{-4m}{-4} = \frac{-8}{-4}$$

$$m = 2$$

Let's substitute m = 2 back into the original equation to verify if it satisfies the equation:

Original equation:

$$-3m - m = -8$$

Substitute m = 2:

$$-3(2) - 2 = -8$$

simplify:

$$-6 - 2 = -8$$

$$-8 = -8$$

Since the equation simplifies to 8 = 8, it confirms that our solution m = 2 is correct.

Equations (Two Sides)

A two-sided equation is an equation where both sides have expressions with variables and constants. The goal when solving a two-sided equation is to find the value of the variable that makes both sides equal.

For example: Let's solve an equation:

$$9 + 8x + 8 = 64 + x + 2$$

Combine Like Terms: Simplify each side of the equation by combining like terms (terms with the same variable or constants).

$$9 + 8x + 8 = 64 + x + 2$$
$$17 + 8x = 66 + x$$

- **Isolate the Variable:** Use inverse operations to isolate the variable on one side of the equation.

subtract x from both sides:

$$17 + 8x - x = 66 + x - x$$

$$17 + 7x = 66$$

subtracting 17 from both sides:

$$17 - 17 + 7x = 66 - 17$$

$$7x = 49$$

divide both sides by 7:

$$\frac{7x}{7} = \frac{49}{7} = x = 7$$

- **Check Solution:** Once you find the solution, substitute it back into the original equation to ensure it makes the equation true.

Substitute $x = 7$ back into the original equation:

$$9 + 8(7) + 8 = 64 + 7 + 2$$

$$9 + 56 + 8 = 64 + 7 + 2$$

$$73 = 73$$

Find Numbers (Verbal Algebra)

Verbal algebra involves translating word problems or verbal statements into algebraic expressions or equations.

For example: The product of the two numbers is 91. One number is six less than the other. What are the numbers?

We're given a verbal description of a problem, and we need to represent it using algebraic symbols and equations.

Let's break down the given problem into algebraic expressions:

- Given that the product of the two numbers is 91, we can write the equation: $xy = 91$
- Also, given that one number is six less than the other, we can write another equation: $x = y - 6$

Now, we can use algebraic techniques to solve the system of equations to find the values of x and y, which represent the two numbers.

$$x(x - 6) = 91$$

1. Solve the equation:

   - Expand the equation:

   $$x^2 - 6x = 91$$

   - Rearrange the equation into standard quadratic form:

   $$x^2 - 6x - 91 = 0$$

   - Factor the quadratic equation:

   $$(x - 13)(x + 7) = 0$$

2. Find the solutions for x.

- From the factored form, we have two possible values for x.

$$x = 13 \text{ or } x = -7$$

3. **Check the validity of the solutions:**

    - Since one number is six less than the other, we discard the negative solution.

    - Therefore, the solution is $x = 13$.

4. **Find the other number:**

    - Substitute $x = 13$ into the expression for the other number:

    Other number $= x - 6 = 13 - 6 = 7$

So, the two numbers are 13 and 7.

Simplifying Expressions

It involves combining like terms and performing operations to make the expression easier to understand and work with.

Let's simplify the expression:

$$2x - 2x + 8 + 4$$

- **Combine like terms:** First, we look for terms with the same variable and exponent. In this expression, $2x$ and $-2x$ are like terms, so they can be combined:

$$2x - 2x = 0$$

- **Substitute the simplified terms:** After combining the like terms, the expression becomes:

$$0 + 8 + 4$$

- **Combine the remaining terms:** Now, we add the constants together:

$$8 + 4 = 12$$

Let's solve another problem:

$$-7m - 3 - 3 - 6m$$

combine like terms

$$-7m - 6m - 3 - 3$$

$$13m - 6$$

Linear Equation

A linear equation is an algebraic equation that represents a straight line when graphed on a coordinate plane. It consists of variables raised to the power of 1 (i.e., no exponents higher than 1) and constant coefficients.

The general form of a linear equation in one variable x is:

$$ax + b = 0$$

Where a and b are constants, and x is the variable.

Let's solve the linear equation:

$$-2x + 9 = 5$$

- **Isolate the variable term:** We want to isolate the term containing x on one side of the equation. To do this, we'll move the constant term to the other side. Subtract 9 from both sides:

$$-2x + 9 - 9 = 5 - 9$$

$$-2x = -4$$

Divide by the coefficient of the variable: To solve for x, divide both sides by the coefficient of x, which is -2:

$$\frac{-2x}{-2} = \frac{-4}{-2}$$

$$x = 2$$

Slop from Two Points

The slope between two points on a Cartesian coordinate system is a measure of the steepness of the line connecting those points. It's calculated by finding the change in the y-coordinates divided by the change in the x-coordinates.

- The coordinates of the first point as $(x_1, y_1) = (2, -30)$.

- The coordinates of the second point as $(x_2, y_2) = (-5, 40)$.

The formula to calculate the slope (m) between two points:

$$\frac{y2 - y1}{x2 - x1}$$

$$= \frac{40 - (-30)}{-5 - 2} = \frac{70}{-7}$$

$$\text{Slope} = -10$$

Graphing Linear Equation

Graphing a linear equation involves plotting the points that satisfy the equation on a coordinate plane and connecting them to form a straight line. Linear equations are equations of the form $y = mx + b$, where m represents the slope of the line, and b represents the y-intercept, the point where the line intersects the y-axis.

To graph a linear equation:

1. Identify the slope (m) and y-intercept (b) from the equation.

2. Plot the y-intercept $(0,b)$) as a point on the y-axis.

3. Use the slope to find additional points on the line. The slope represents the change in y for every unit change in x.

4. Connect the points to form a straight line.

For example, to graph the equation:

$$y = \frac{9}{4}x - 8$$

1. **Identify the slope and y-intercept:** The slope is $\frac{9}{4}$, and the y-intercept is -8.

2. **Plot the y-intercept:** Plot the point $(0,-8)$.

3. **Use the slope to plot additional points:** the slop is $\frac{9}{4}$ to find another point. we will move up 9 units and 4 units to the right from the y-intercept to find another point.

4. **Draw the line:** Once we have at least two points, we can draw a straight line.

We can continue this process to plot more points and extend the line further if needed.

$$y = \frac{9}{4}x - 8$$

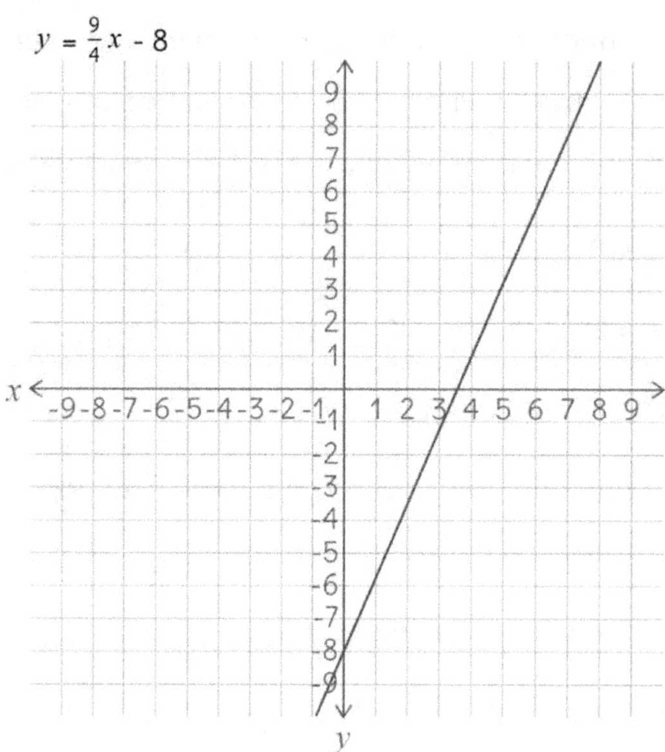

Quadratic Equations

A quadratic equation is a polynomial equation of the second degree, meaning it can be written in the form:

$$ax^2 + bx + c = 0$$

where a, b, and c are constants, and x is the variable being solved for. The solutions to a quadratic equation are the values of x that make the equation true.

Now, let's solve the quadratic equation $11x^2 - 1 = 0$ and understand it step by step using quadratic formula.

1. **Identify the coefficients:**

    In the equation $11x^2 - 1 = 0$,

$$a=11, b=0, \text{ and } c=-1.$$

2. **Apply the quadratic formula:**

    The quadratic formula states that for an equation $ax^2 + bx + c = 0$, the solutions for x are given by:

$$x = \frac{-b \pm \sqrt{b^2 - 4ac}}{2a}$$

    Plugging in the values a=11, b=0, and c=−1 into the quadratic formula, we get:

$$x = \frac{-0 \pm \sqrt{0 - 4(11)(-1)}}{2(11)}$$

3. Simplify inside the square root:

$$0^2 - 4(11)(-1) = 0 - (-44) = 44$$

4. Plug in the simplified values:

$$x = \frac{\pm\sqrt{44}}{22}$$

5. Simplify the square root:

Since 44 is not a perfect square, we can write it as $\sqrt[2]{11}$

$$x = \frac{\pm\sqrt[2]{11}}{22}$$

6. Simplify further if possible:

We can simplify $\sqrt[2]{11}$ to $\sqrt{11}$ by canceling out the common factor:

$$x = \frac{\pm\sqrt{11}}{11}$$

7. Final solution:

So, the solutions to the equation are:

$$x = \frac{\sqrt{11}}{11} \text{ and } x = \frac{-\sqrt{11}}{11}$$

or

$$(x = 0.302, \text{ and } x = -0.302)$$

These are the roots of the quadratic equation. They represent the points where the graph of the quadratic equation intersects the x-axis.

Let's solve another equation:

$$-4p^2 + 6p - 6 = 0$$

$$p = \frac{-b \pm \sqrt{b^2 - 4ac}}{2a}$$

where $a = -4$, $b = 6$, and $c = -6$.

Let's plug these values into the quadratic formula:

$$p = \frac{-6 \pm \sqrt{6^2 - 4(-4)(-6)}}{2(-4)}$$

First, let's simplify inside the square root:

$$6^2 - 4(-4)(-6)$$

$$= 36 - 96 = -60$$

So, we have:

$$p = \frac{-6 \pm \sqrt{-60}}{-8}$$

We can simplify the square root of −60 by factoring out −1:

$$\sqrt{-60}$$

$$= \sqrt{-1 \times 60}$$

$$= \sqrt{-1} \times \sqrt{60}$$

$$= i\sqrt{60}$$

So, we have:

$$p = \frac{-6 \pm i\sqrt{60}}{-8}$$

Simplify:

$$\sqrt{60} \text{ to } \sqrt{4 \times 15} = 2\sqrt{15}$$

$$p = \frac{-6 \pm i \times 2\sqrt{15}}{-8}$$

Now, divide both the numerator and denominator by −2 to simplify:

$$p = \frac{3 \pm i\sqrt{15}}{4}$$

So, the solutions to the equation are:

$$p = \frac{3 + i\sqrt{15}}{4} \quad \text{and} \quad p = \frac{3 - i\sqrt{15}}{4}$$

This equation $-4p^2 + 6p - 6 = 0$ has no real solutions.

When a quadratic equation has no real solutions, it means that the solutions are not real numbers, but rather complex numbers. In this case, the solutions involve the imaginary unit i because the discriminant ($b^2 - 4ac$) is negative, which results in taking the square root of a negative number when applying the quadratic formula.

In mathematics, such equations are said to have "no real roots" or "no real solutions." They are also sometimes referred to as having "complex roots" or "complex solutions." Complex numbers include a real part and an imaginary part, and they are often written in the form $a + bi$, where a and b are real numbers and i is the imaginary unit, defined as $i = \sqrt{-1}$.

Let's solve another equation:

$$12x^2 + 6x - 2 = 0$$

$$x = \frac{-b \pm \sqrt{b^2 - 4ac}}{2a}$$

where $a = 12$, $b = 6$, and $c = -2$.

Let's plug these values into the quadratic formula:

$$x = \frac{-6 \pm \sqrt{6^2 - 4(12)(-2)}}{2(12)}$$

First, let's simplify inside the square root:

$$6^2 - 4(12)(-2)$$

$$= 36 - (-96)$$

$$= 36 + 96$$

$$= 132$$

So, we have:

$$X = \frac{-6 \pm \sqrt{132}}{24}$$

Now, let's simplify the square root of 132:

$$X = \frac{-6 \pm \sqrt{4 \times 33}}{24}$$

$$X = \frac{-6 \pm 2\sqrt{33}}{24}$$

$$X = \frac{-6 \pm \sqrt{33}}{12}$$

So, the solutions to the equation are:

$$X = \frac{-6 + \sqrt{33}}{12} \text{ and } X = \frac{-6 - \sqrt{33}}{12}$$

or (x = 0.229, and x = -0.729)

Let's solve a quadratic equation where the right side is a number, instead of 0.

$$-8n^2 + 6n + 30 = 7$$

To solve the equation, we first need to bring all terms to one side to set the equation equal to zero:

$$-8n^2 + 6n + 30 - 7 = 0$$

Simplify:

$$-8n^2 + 6n + 23 = 0$$

Now, to solve for n, we can use the quadratic formula:

$$n = \frac{-b \pm \sqrt{b^2 - 4ac}}{2a}$$

where $a = -8$, $b = 6$, and $c = 23$.

Plugging these values into the formula, we get:

$$n = \frac{-6 \pm \sqrt{6^2 - 4(-8)(23)}}{2(-8)}$$

$$n = \frac{-6 \pm \sqrt{36 + 736}}{-16}$$

$$n = \frac{-6 \pm \sqrt{772}}{-16}$$

Now, let's simplify the square root of 772. We can factor out 4:

$$\sqrt{772} = \sqrt{4 \times 193} = 2\sqrt{193}$$

So, our equation becomes:

$$n = \frac{-6 \pm 2\sqrt{193}}{-8}$$

So, the solutions to the equation are:

$$n = \frac{-3 + \sqrt{193}}{-8} \text{ and } n = \frac{-3 - \sqrt{193}}{-8}$$

or

(n = -1.362, and n = 2.112)

Polynomials

A polynomial is an algebraic expression consisting of one or more terms, where each term is a constant, a variable, or a product of constants and variables raised to whole number exponents.

Examples of polynomials include:

- $(7v^2 + 2v^4) + (8v^2 + 4v^4)$
- $(2v + 4v^2 + 2) - (5v - 4v^4 - 6v^2)$
- $(7x - 5\,y)(2x - 6\,y)$
- $(6x^2 + 4xy + 6\,y^2)(8x^2 + 3xy + 3\,y^2)$
- $\dfrac{2x^3 + 8x^2 + 2x}{2x^2}$

Operations on Polynomials

Addition of Polynomials:

- To add polynomials, simply combine like terms.
- Like terms are terms that have the same variable(s) raised to the same power(s).
- For example, to add $3x^2 + 2x$ and $5x^2 - 7x$, group the like terms: $3x^2 + 5x^2$ and $2x - 7x$, then add each group separately.

Subtraction of Polynomials:

- To subtract polynomials, distribute the negative sign and then add.
- For example, to subtract $x^2 - 2x$ from $4x^2 + 3x$, distribute the negative sign to each term in the second polynomial: $-(x^2 - 2x)$, then add each term separately.

Solving Two-Step Equations

Solve for the variable.

1. $-6\dfrac{y}{-9} = 6$

2. $-10\dfrac{-k}{1} = 40$

3. $6\dfrac{-z}{1} = -6$

4. $-7 = -b - 6$

5. $\dfrac{1+y}{1} = 9$

6. $6 + \dfrac{m}{3} = 8$

7. $10(-4 + z) = -10$

8. $3 = (1 + m) - 8$

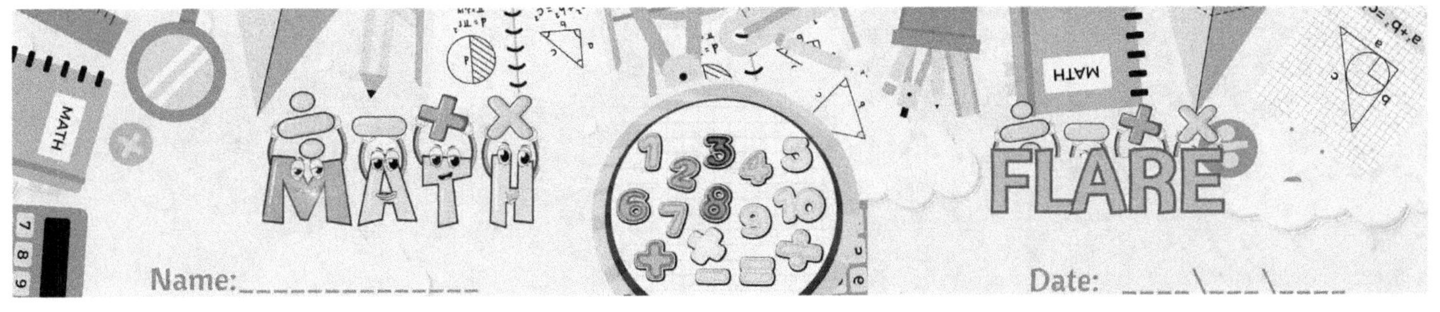

9. $11 = 10 + \dfrac{z}{10}$

10. $(9 + k) - 6 = 7$

11. $4s + 5 = 13$

12. $\dfrac{10 + s}{-4} = -2.8$

13. $9 = 1(6 + k)$

14. $\dfrac{y}{4} - 4 = -2$

15. $4(7 + a) = 60$

16. $-5(-1 + y) = -5$

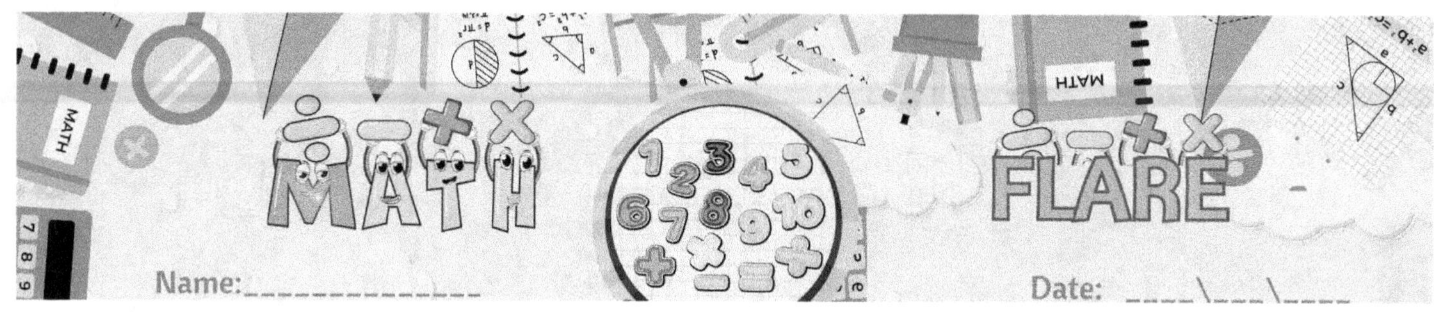

17. $70 = (8 + y)7$

18. $36 = -9(-10 + x)$

19. $-7 = \dfrac{m}{4} - 9$

20. $8(2 - z) = -32$

21. $\dfrac{b}{8} + 10 = 11$

22. $-3 = 1\dfrac{-s}{3}$

23. $-1.9 = \dfrac{6 + z}{-8}$

24. $(10 + z)9 = 162$

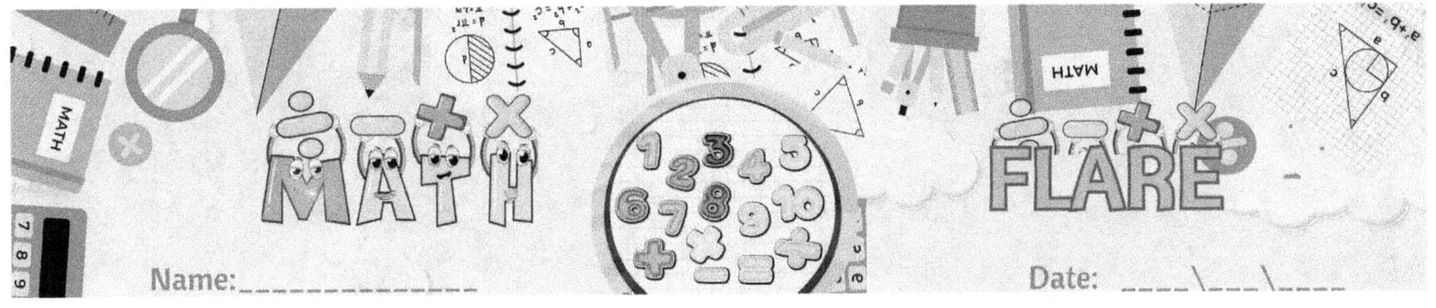

25. $\dfrac{a}{2} + 1 = 6$

26. $18 = \dfrac{y}{1} + 10$

27. $-86 = -10z - 6$

28. $-5(-7 + y) = 15$

29. $5(-5 + m) = 20$

30. $-26 = -6a - 8$

31. $4 = 1\dfrac{b}{2}$

32. $100 = 10(1 + s)$

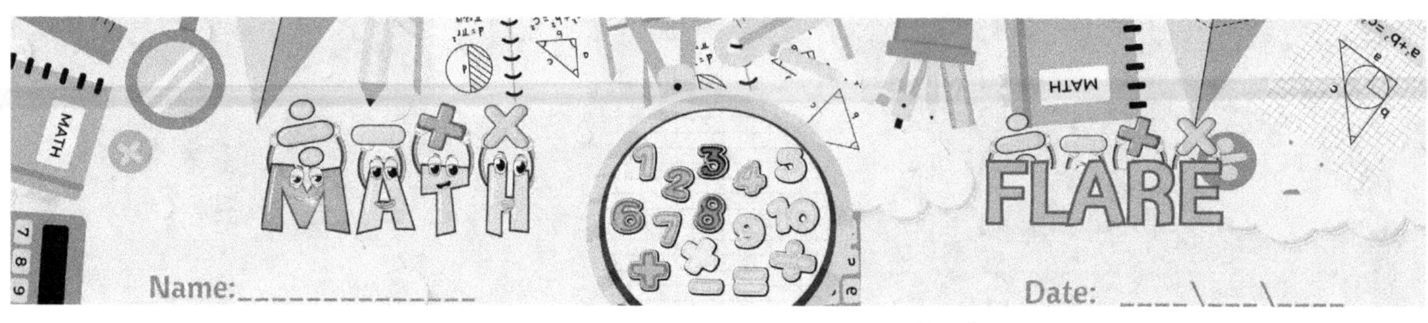

33. $-1(-8 + m) = 0$

34. $-4.8 = \dfrac{9 + k}{-4}$

35. $9 = \dfrac{8 + m}{1}$

36. $(1 - b) - 6 = -11$

37. $-3 = (5 - y)1$

38. $\dfrac{-6 + a}{1} = -5$

39. $0 = -7(-6 + z)$

40. $4 = (4 + k) - 8$

41. $10 = 10\dfrac{a}{9}$

42. $-90 = (1 - m)10$

43. $\dfrac{8 + b}{-10} = -1.2$

44. $-45 = -3(5 + k)$

45. $7(1 - b) = -56$

46. $\dfrac{m}{2} - 9 = -7$

47. $-1.9 = \dfrac{8 + x}{-9}$

48. $-4 = \dfrac{-8 + b}{1}$

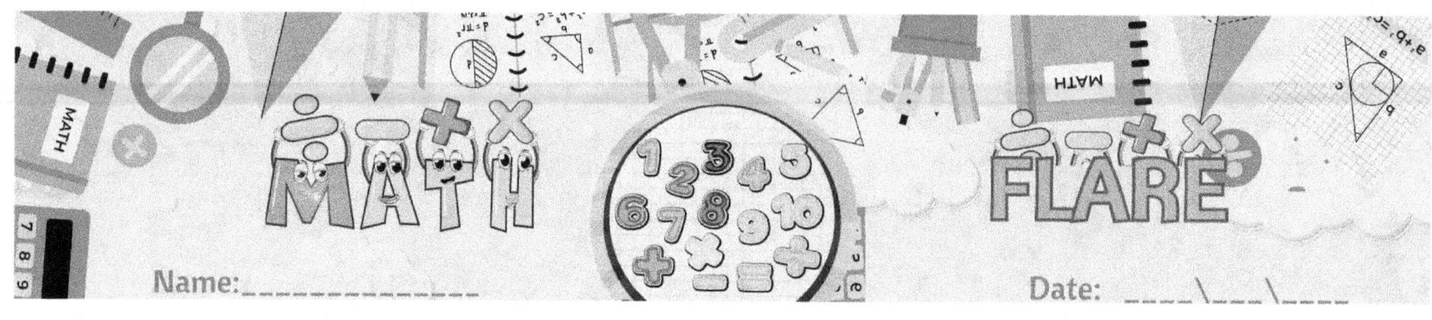

Solving Multi-Step Equations

Solve for the variable.

1. $112 = 2 + z + 10z$

2. $-8 - 2a - 3 = -23$

3. $-a + 10 + 10a = 55$

4. $1 + 5y + 2y = 57$

5. $-3 = 5 - x - x$

6. $21 = 9m - 3 + 6$

7. $-42 = -10x - 5 - 7$

8. $6 = -1 + x + 2$

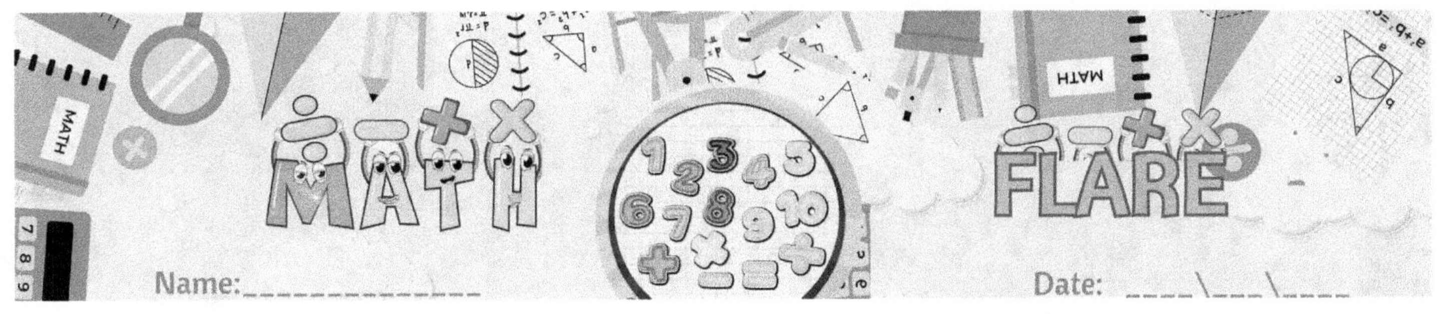

9. $-4 - y - y = -22$

10. $-2 - s - s = -4$

11. $32 = 4k + 7 + k$

12. $-9 - s + 8s = 33$

13. $-18 = 10 - z - 3z$

14. $4 + 5a - 9a = -36$

15. $0 = -3k + 3k$

16. $7 = -a + 7 + a$

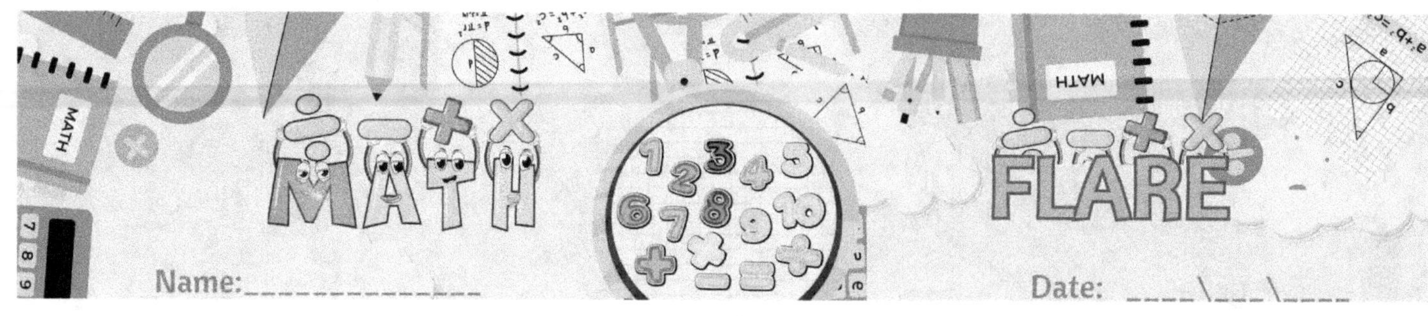

17. $20 = -2 + 2a + 6$

18. $1 - 2a - 8 = -19$

19. $3 + z + z = 15$

20. $-y - 8y = -27$

21. $-2z + 9 + z = 8$

22. $4 + z - 7z = -56$

23. $12 = -6 - z + 4z$

24. $-10 - y - 2 = -14$

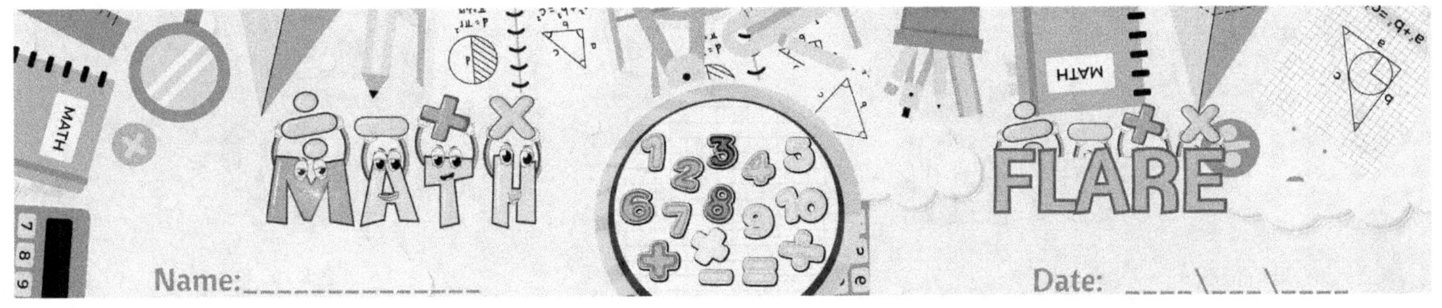

25. $-2z - z = -9$

26. $10m + 8 + m = 30$

27. $5 = -4 + 2a - 9$

28. $z - 10 - 6z = -40$

29. $-70 = -8a + a$

30. $-10 + 7m + 2 = -1$

31. $3 + a + 2a = 12$

32. $-13 = -8x + 5 - x$

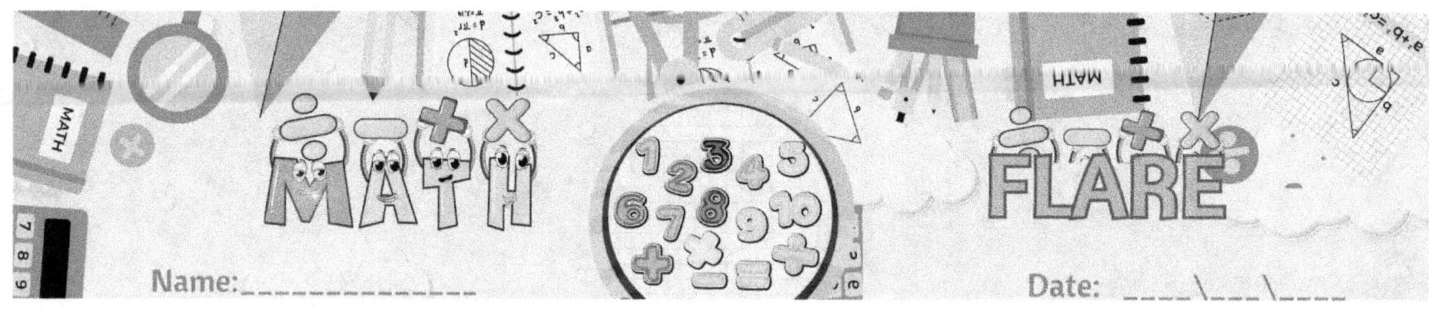

33. $-5 = -9 - 2s + 6s$

34. $-6 - 9y + 5y = -38$

35. $10x + 5x = 15$

36. $24 = 6x - 4 + x$

37. $-29 = -3x + 2 - 10$

38. $-4 + 6k + 8 = 64$

39. $-49 = 3 - 7s - 10$

40. $-b + 9 + 8b = 30$

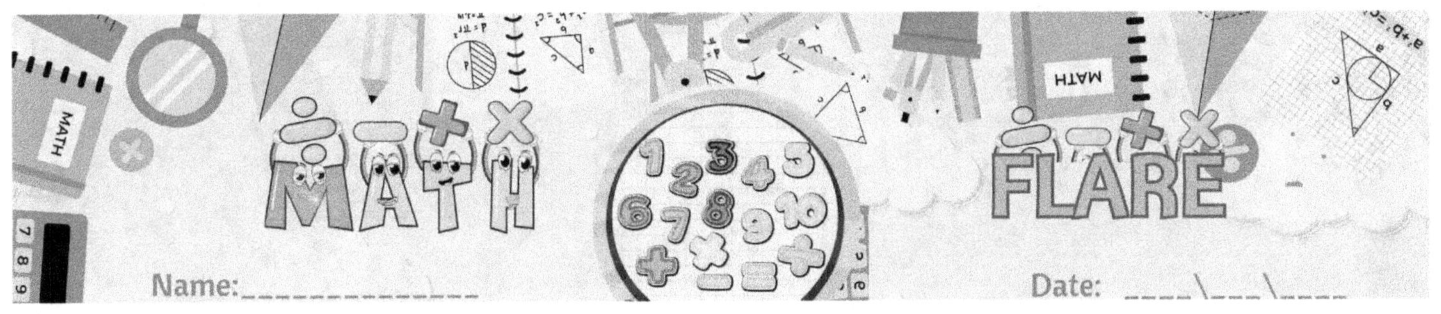

41. $-55 = -10 - 10b + b$

42. $-7 = -6m + 7 + 4$

43. $-32 = 6 - 3b - 8$

44. $5 - y - 8y = -58$

45. $25 = 6x - 3 + x$

46. $-7 + 9k - 1 = 46$

47. $-13 = -3x + 7 - x$

48. $a - 2 - 9a = -42$

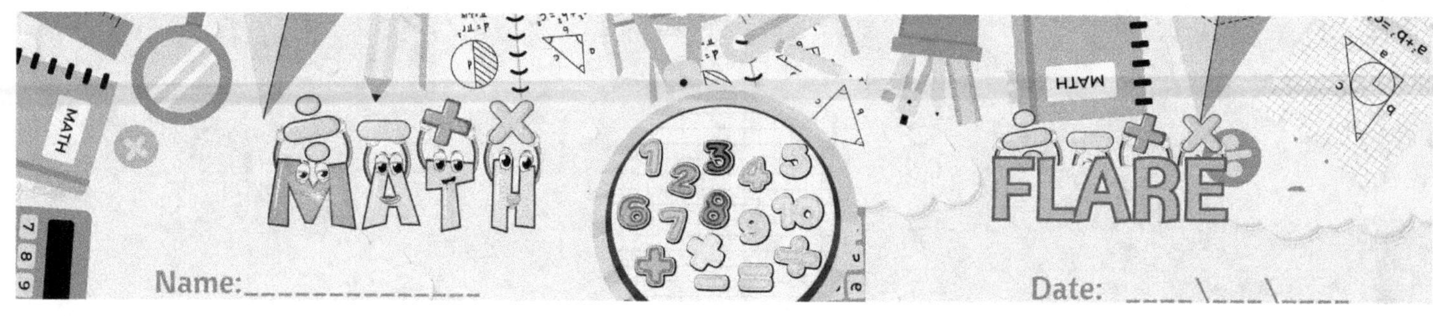

49. $30 = -4s + 7s$

50. $-6m + 8m = 20$

51. $-21 = -10 - a - 10a$

52. $-65 = -6x - 2 - x$

53. $-8 = -7y + 6 + 7$

54. $58 = 4 + 8m + m$

55. $-4 = 6m - 3 - 7$

56. $50 = 7x - 2x$

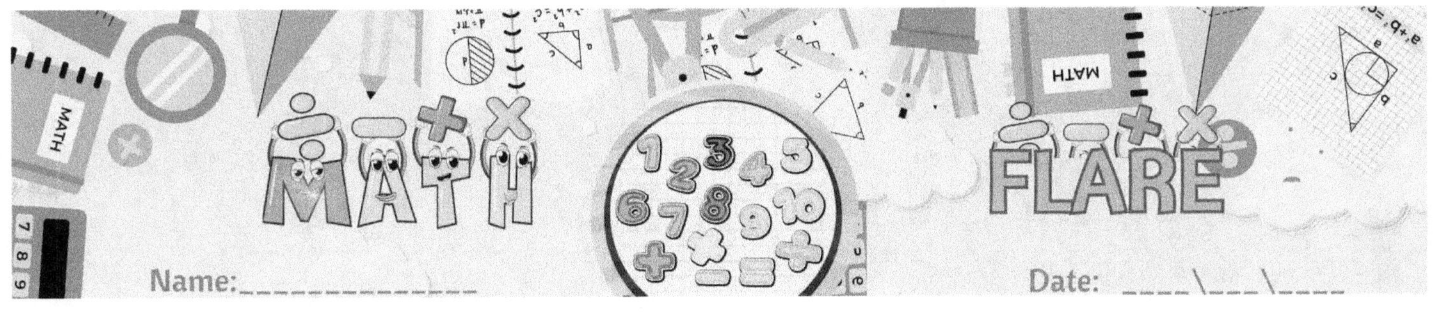

Equations (Two Sides)
Solve for the variable.

1. $99 + x = -10x$

2. $2 - x = 5 + -3x + -9$

3. $-5 + -4m + 5 = -18 - m$

4. $-7 + 8z = -133 + -10z$

5. $-5z + -4 = 8 + z$

6. $2a + -1 = 14 - a$

7. $66 + b = -1 + -10b + -10$

8. $-1 + 9b = -41 + b$

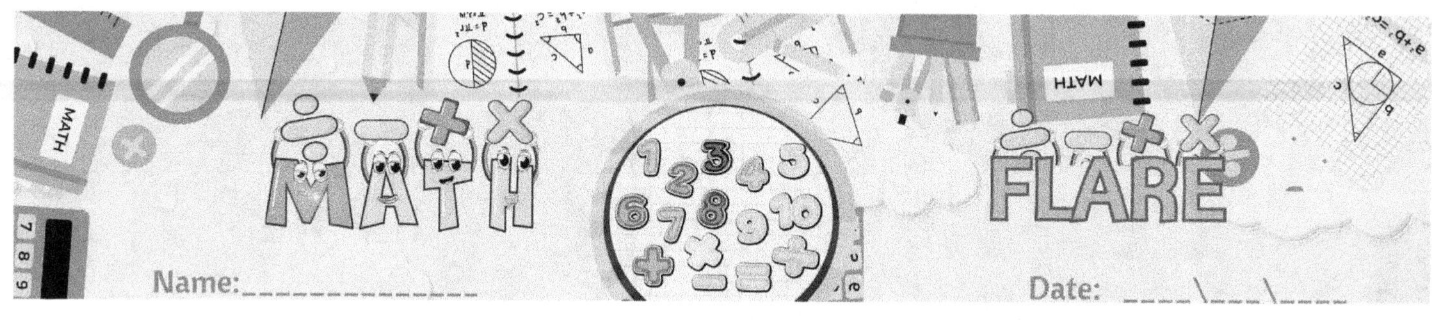

9. $4 + -4k + -4 = -5 + k$

10. $0 + k + -1 = 2 + 3k + -9$

11. $9a + -5 = -9a + 85$

12. $-6b = -20 - b$

13. $27 - b + -4 = 6 + 7b + -7$

14. $-8 - a = -4 + 3a + -8$

15. $7 + -8a = 63 - a$

16. $-27 + -2z = 9 + 7z$

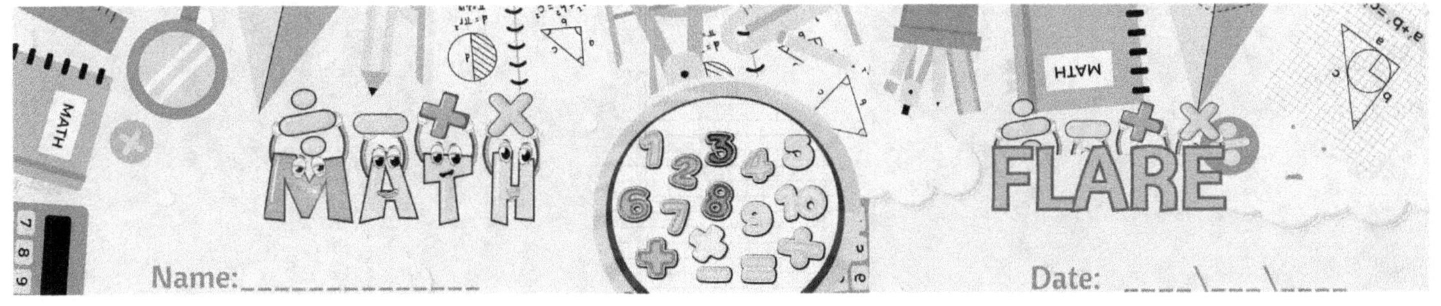

17. $10 + y = 1 + -8y$

18. $-8 + 8z + -9 = 46 - z$

19. $-7 + -8x + 10 = 90 - x + -17$

20. $-21 - z = -3z + -5$

21. $-10 + 6s = 4s + -2$

22. $12 + m = -5m$

23. $8z = -45 - z$

24. $1k + 1 = 0 - -2k$

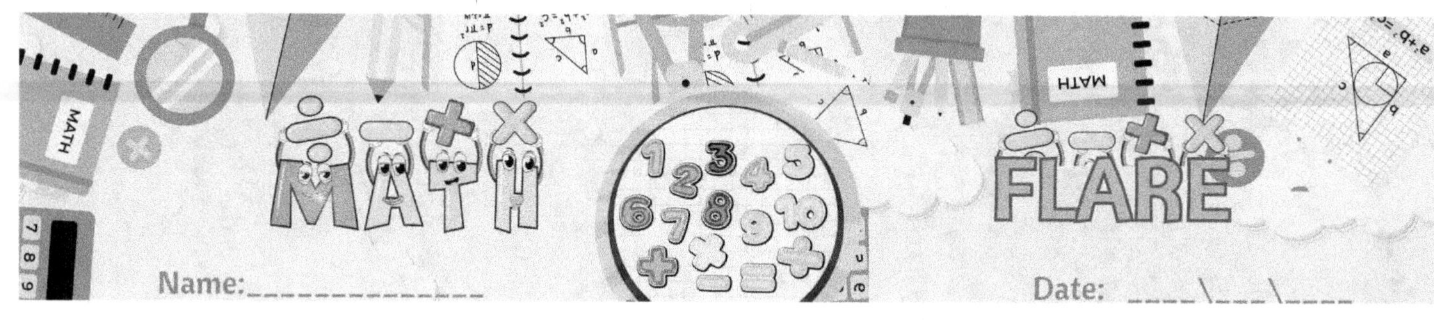

25. $-38 - y = 7y + 10$

26. $-21 - s = 2s$

27. $5z = 36 - z$

28. $-7 + -9a + -3 = -97 + a + -13$

29. $-4x + -4 = -19 - x$

30. $30 - z = 8 + -5z + -2$

31. $-63 - y = -8y$

32. $-63 - 6s = 8s + -7$

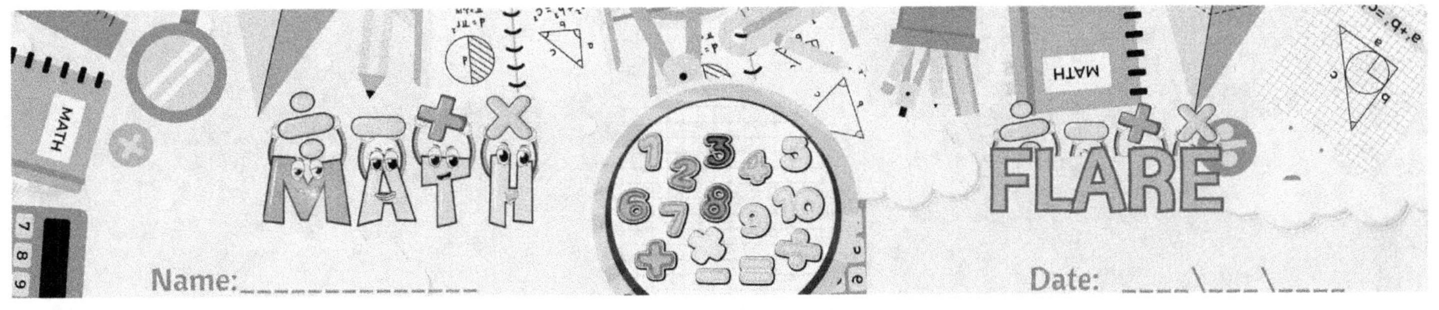

33. $-2 + -6k + 2 = -14 + k + 0$

34. $45 - y = 4y$

35. $-18 - s = -10 + 4s + 2$

36. $-4z = 20 + z$

37. $-13 + z = 6 + -2z + -7$

38. $-10z + 4 = -62 + z$

39. $6 - k + -2 = -2 + -8k + -1$

40. $29 + a = 8a + -6$

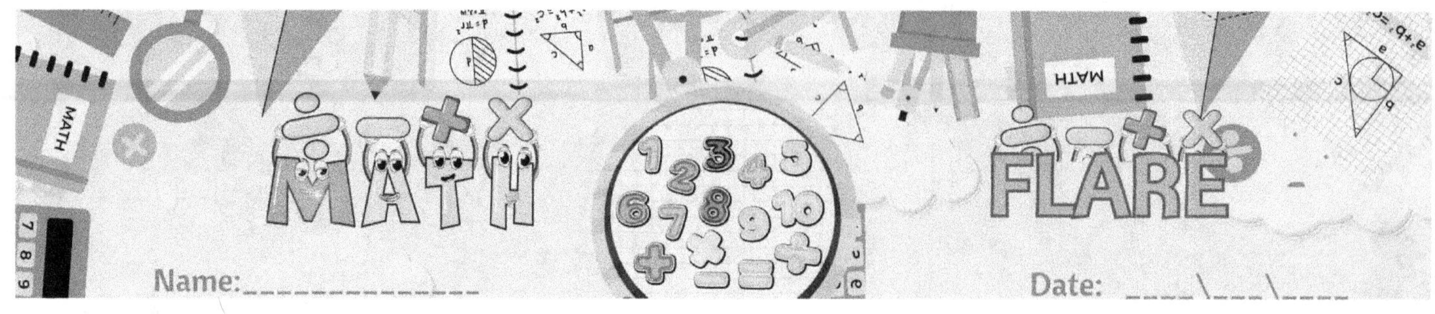

41. $17 - z + 10 = 1 + 2z + 2$

42. $-6 + 9s + -1 = -47 - s$

43. $-9a = -50 + a$

44. $-72 + x = 9x$

45. $5 + 6y + 8 = 2 - y + 4$

46. $4 + -9x + 5 = 25 - x$

47. $-3 + 2z + 7 = 11 + z + 0$

48. $2 + -5b + 3 = -2 - b + 3$

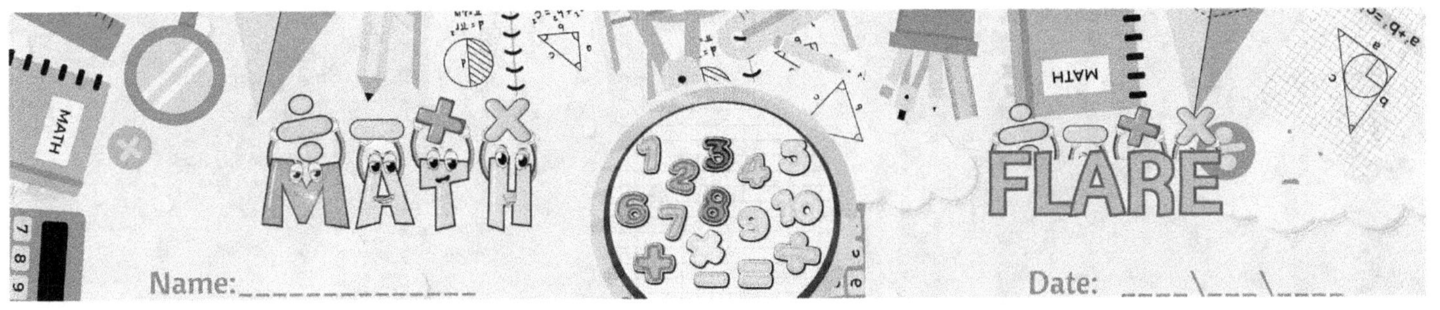

49. $2m = -30 - m$

50. $-25 + m = 5 + -9m$

51. $-7b = 80 + b$

52. $-77 + s + 12 = 2 + 7s + -7$

53. $-24 - y = 3y$

54. $-79 - 3b = 6b + -7$

55. $40 - x = -6x$

56. $-8b + 10 = 28 + b$

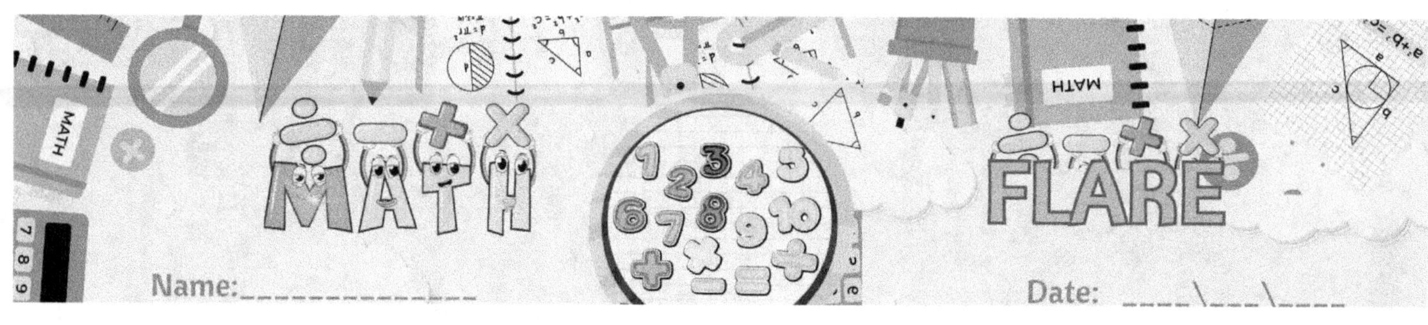

Simplify Expressions

1. $-8y - 10 - 3y$

2. $14 + 13z - z + 1 - 16z$

3. $-2 - 3m + 13 - 13m$

4. $2z + z$

5. $10 + 6m - 16m + 19 - 8m$

6. $6 + 6z - 3 + 18z$

7. $-17y + 4y + 11 - y$

8. $-7k - 5k$

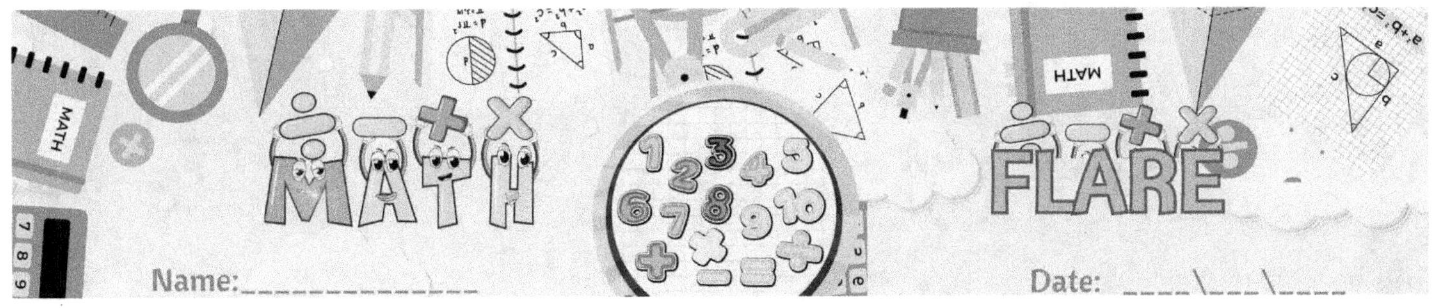

9. $-16y - 13 - 2y$

10. $-18z + 6 + 2z + 4 + 2z - 3$

11. $4 + 16k - 13k$

12. $-18y + 14 + 13y + 9 + 15y - 5$

13. $17k - 11 - 2k + 5 - 6$

14. $13 + k - 3 + 9k$

15. $9z + 7z$

16. $8 + 17(5z - 13)$

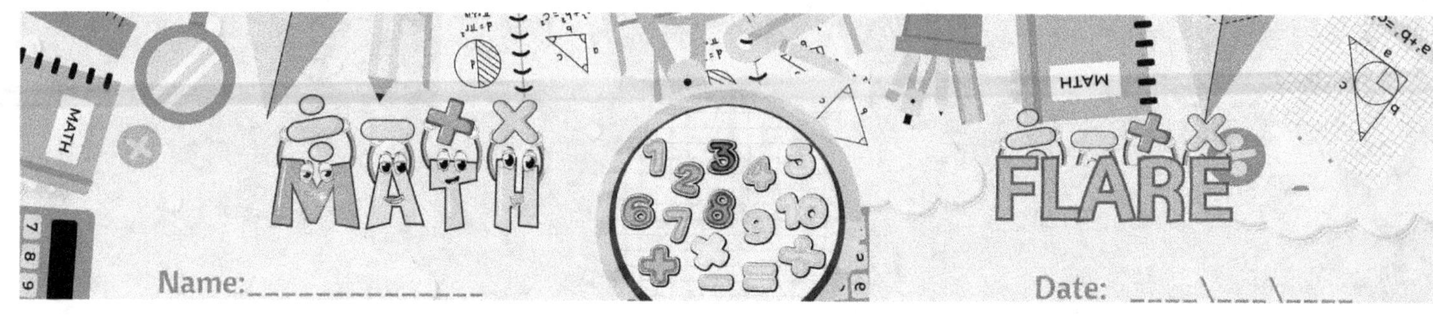

17. $-13x - 3 + 5x$

18. $-15m - 2 - 9 - 3m$

19. $6y + 7 + 14y + 16 + 10y + 12$

20. $3 - 16(-11k + 19)$

21. $1 + 9y - 19y + 15 - 16y$

22. $8 + 3(-6x + 13)$

23. $14 + m - 9m$

24. $2m + 3 + m$

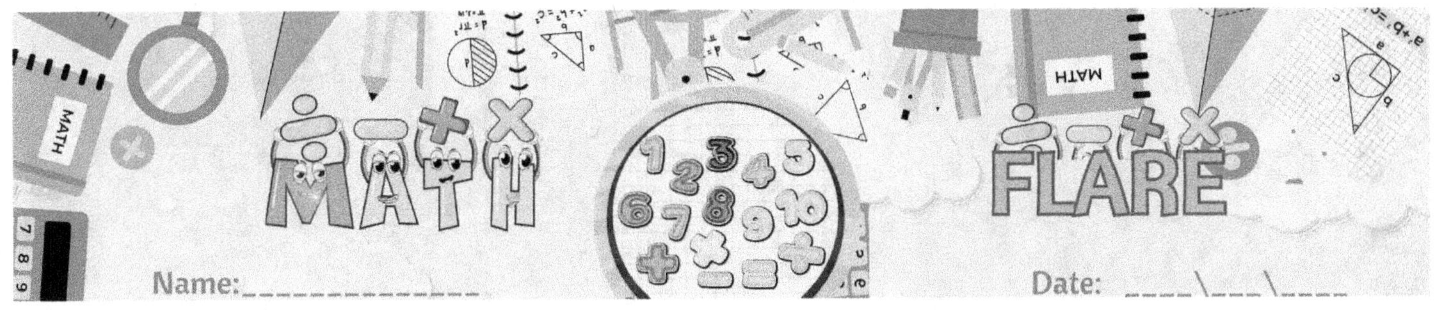

25. $-13z + 17z + 3 - 8z$

26. $-19k + 16 - 14 + 19k$

27. $15y + 2 - 15 - 5y + 14y$

28. $13 + 18(11k + 1)$

29. $3 + 15m - 17m$

30. $-5m + 13 + 13m$

31. $z + 10 + 10z + 13 + 19z + 17$

32. $3y - 2 - 14y + 3$

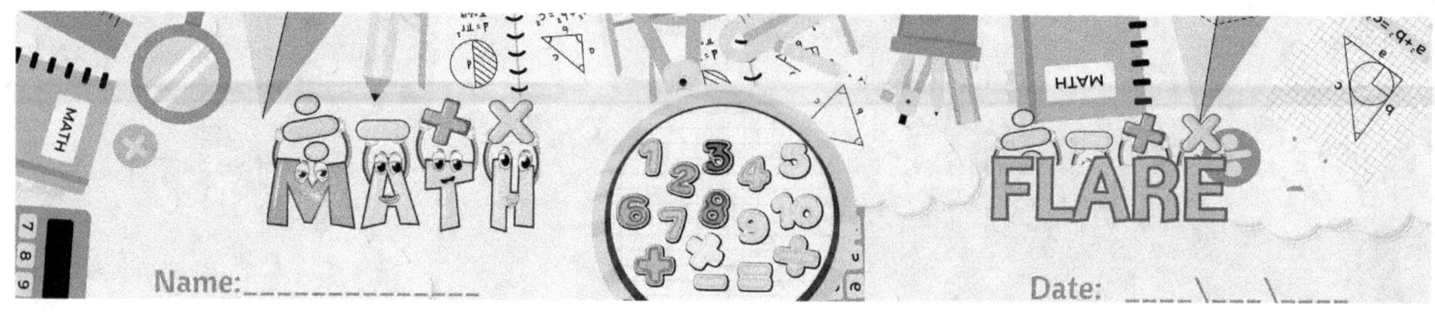

33. $19k + 9 - 8 - 2k + 20k$

34. $-19y + 8y + 3 - 11y$

35. $11k - 3k + 10k - 6 + 11$

36. $-6k + 18k + 4 - 3k$

37. $-13y - 6 - 15y$

38. $9 + 16m - 11m$

39. $-k - 17k$

40. $-18z + 2 + z$

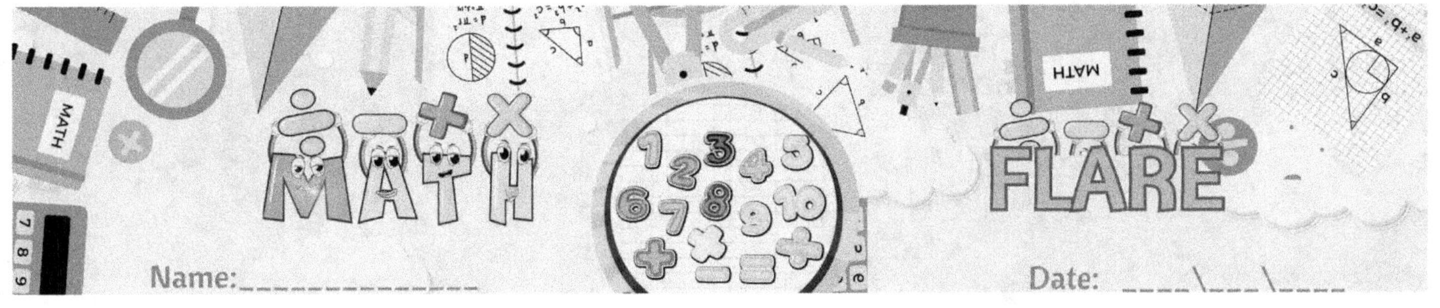

41. $6y - 16 - 6y + 2 - 3$

42. $-5z + 10 + 19z + 3 + 11z - 10$

43. $12y - 13y$

44. $-20k - 20 - 17k$

45. $10 - 11x + 7 - 11x + 4 - 2x$

46. $18m + 15 + m$

47. $-14k - k$

48. $10 - 20z + 11 - 18z + 16 - z$

49. $18k + 9 - 7k + 12 + 19k + 7$

50. $-17 + 18z + 17 - 2z$

51. $4x - 12x + 16 + 17$

52. $10 - 15(-19m + 8)$

53. $-9m - 6 - 18m$

54. $10y + 13y$

55. $-k + 3k + 1 - 19k$

56. $19 + 14m - 17 + 15m$

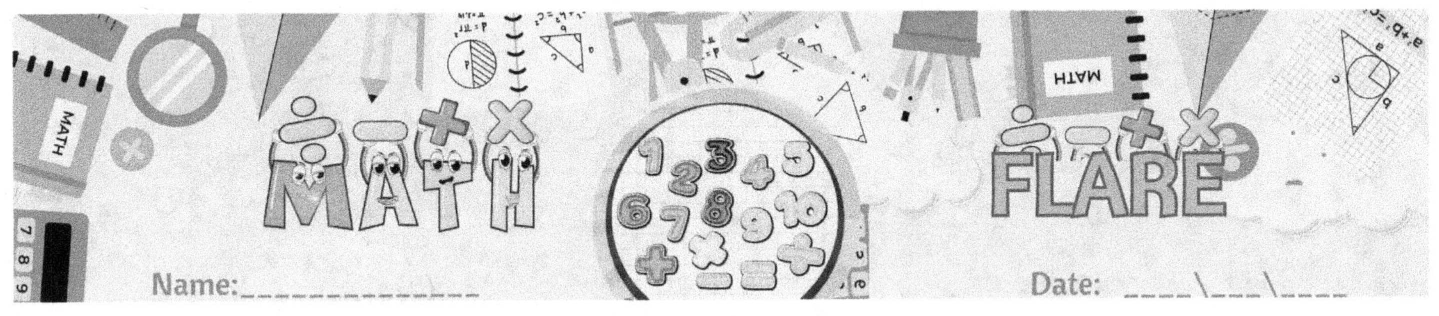

Evaluating Equations

Simplify the following equations when the value of n = -6

1. $(-9n + -9) + (-9n - 2) =$

2. $-8 + -7n =$

3. $-1 + (-10n + 5) - -8 + (8n) =$

4. $5 + (5n + -9) - 2 + (-8n) =$

5. $2^2 + n^1 =$

6. $8 + -4n =$

7. $(-2n + -4) + (5n - 1) =$

8. $-7n + 4 - -9n =$

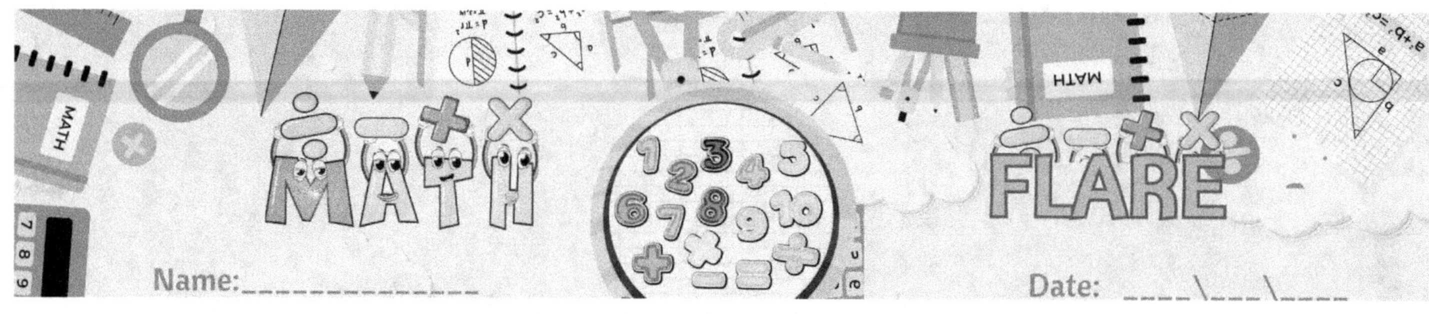

Evaluating Equations

Simplify the following equations when the value of $n = -10$

1. $(0 + 5n) + (-1n - 10) - (4 + -9n) =$

2. $n - -2 =$

3. $0n + 4 =$

4. $(-9n + 6) + (10n + -8) =$

5. $-6 + n =$

6. $4 + (-5n + -4) - -2 + (-8n) =$

7. $8n - n =$

8. $n^1 + n - -4 =$

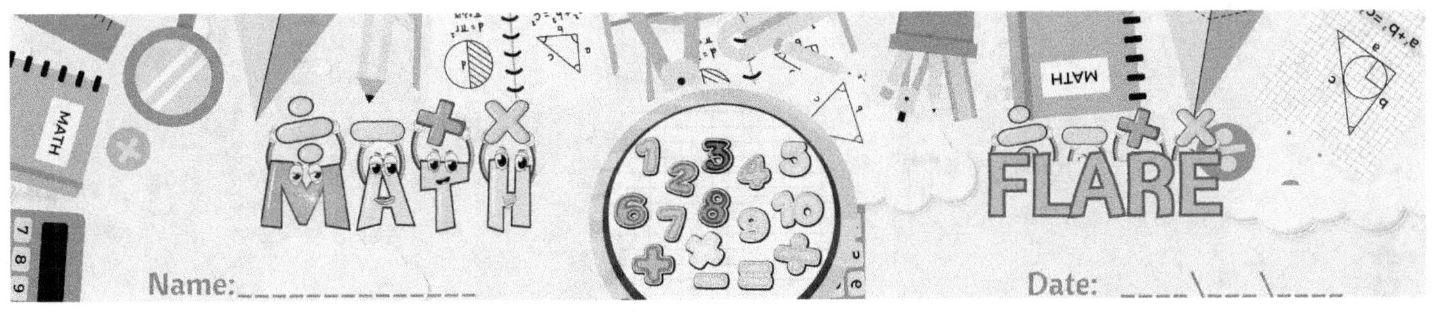

Evaluating Equations

Simplify the following equations when the value of $n = -9$

1. $-9n + -1 - 7n =$

2. $n^3 + n - -9 =$

3. $n^1 + n - -8 =$

4. $-3 + n =$

5. $-8(9 + n) =$

6. $n + 2 + -3n =$

7. $n^3 + n - 9 =$

8. $(n^3 + -6) - 8(-8 + n) =$

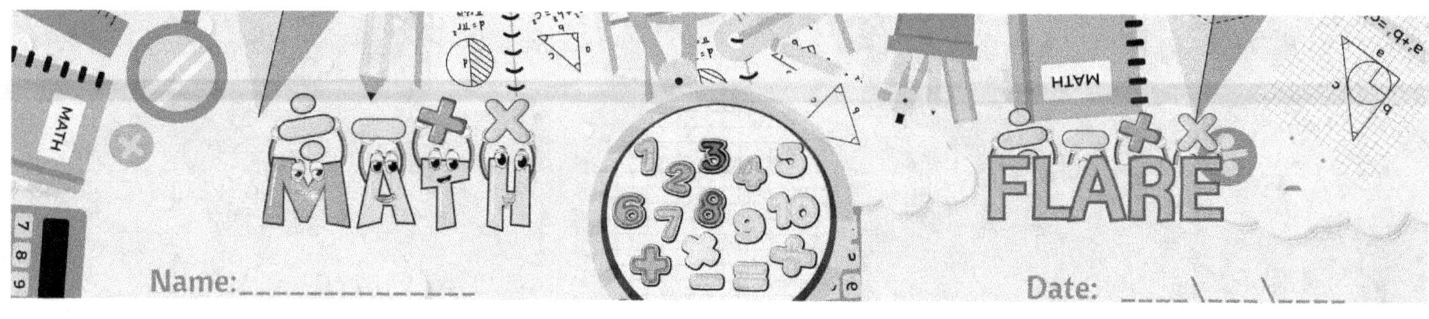

Evaluating Equations

Simplify the following equations when the value of $n = -8$

1. $n^2 + n - -10 =$

2. $4 - n =$

3. $10(7n - 1) + 9(-2 + n) =$

4. $3 + (0n + 1) - 2 + (-10n) =$

5. $-4n + -7n - -9 =$

6. $-8n + -4n - -7 =$

7. $(-2n + 6) + (6n - 10) =$

8. $-8n + 2 =$

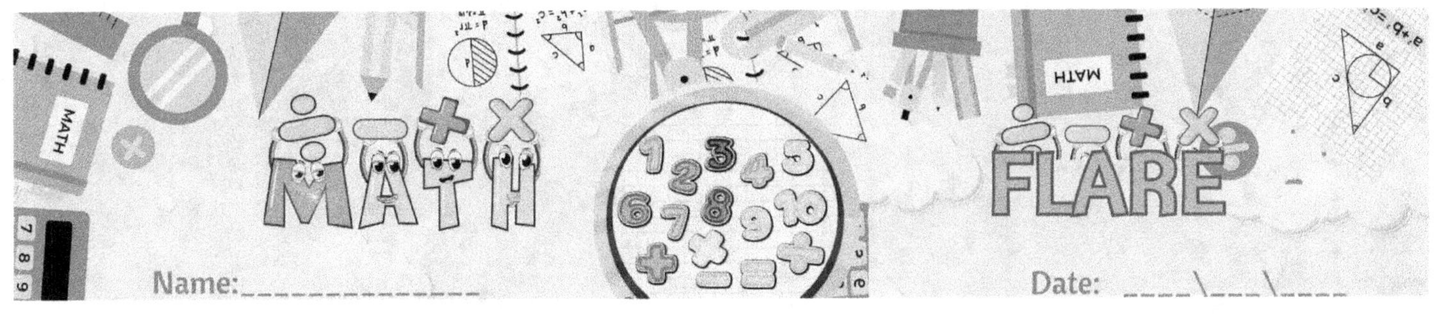

Name:________________   Date: _______________

Evaluating Equations

Simplify the following equations when the value of $n = 4$

1. $8n + -4n + -5n =$

2. $-9n - 1 =$

3. $9n^2 + -7n^2 =$

4. $-4(2 - n) =$

5. $-3n + -6 =$

6. $n^2 + n - -2 =$

7. $(-8 + 6n) + (-2n - 9) - (7 + -1n) =$

8. $-9 - n =$

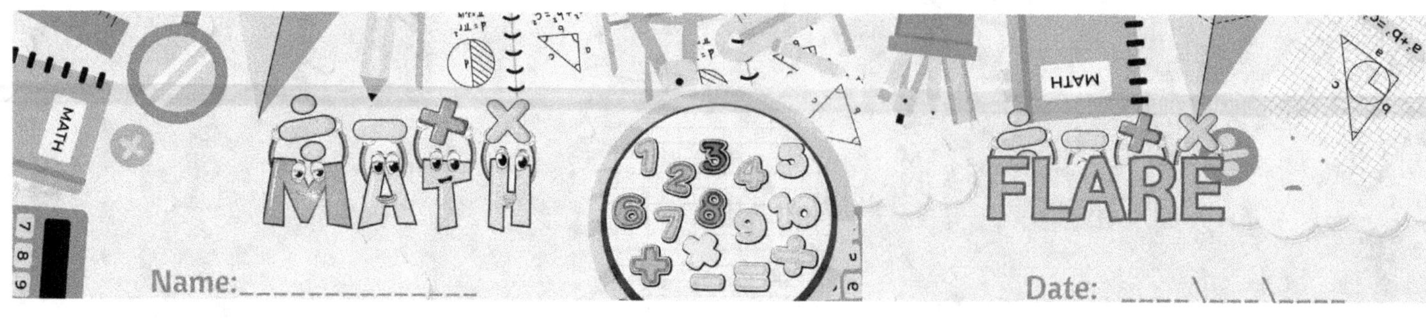

Evaluating Equations

Simplify the following equations when the value of n = 5

1. $-8n + n =$

2. $(8 + -7n) + (n - 2) - (2 + 5n) =$

3. $n + 3 + 0n =$

4. $n - 1 =$

5. $-10 - n =$

6. $10 + (n + -8) =$

7. $-8n - n =$

8. $3 + (6n + 8) =$

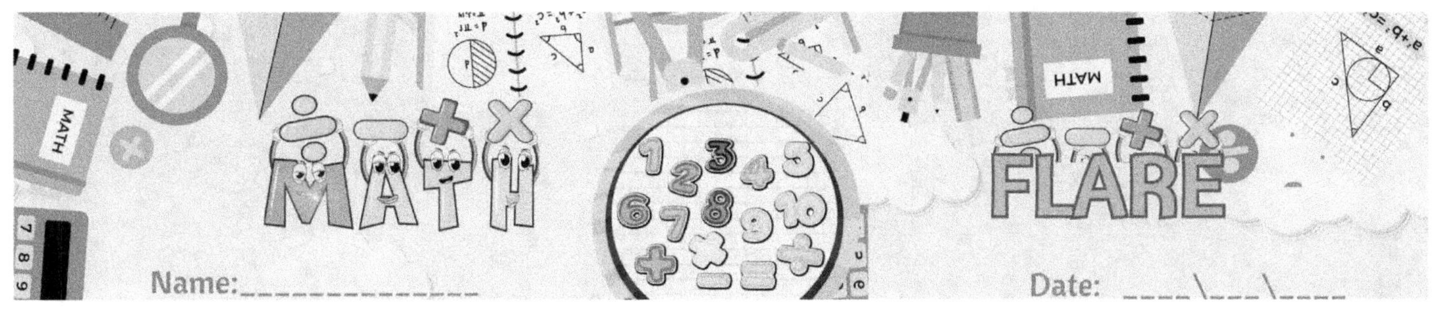

Name:_________________   Date: ______________

Evaluating Equations

Simplify the following equations when the value of n = 7

1. $-2 + \dfrac{49}{n} + -4^3 =$

2. $(-7n)^2 =$

3. $-2n - -4 =$

4. $(n + -4) \div -5 =$

5. $n(-7 + n) =$

6. $5 + \dfrac{7}{n} + -6^3 =$

7. $n^2 + n - 3 =$

8. $6 \div n + -10 =$

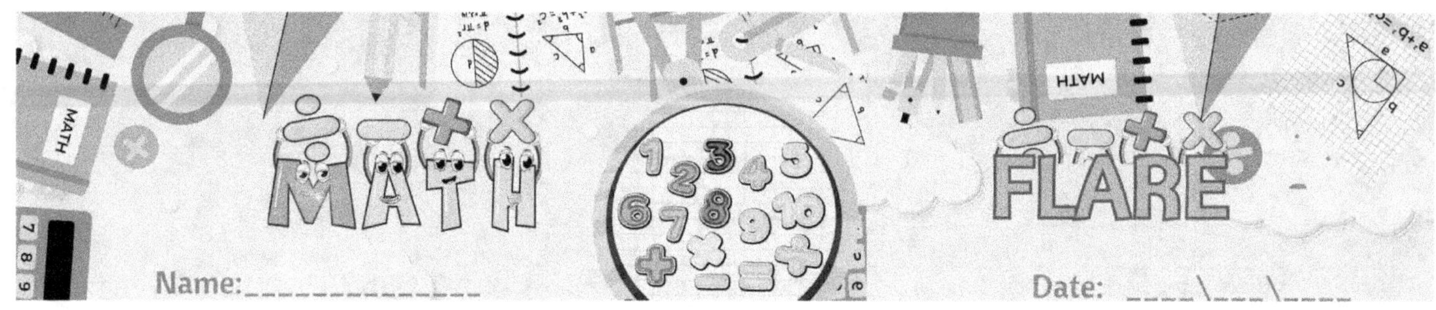

Verbal Algebra Expressions

1. The product of six and a number is 6. What is the number?

2. The greater of two numbers is 10 less than nine times the smaller number. Their sum is 10. Find the numbers.

3. One number is six times another. Their sum is 28. Find the numbers.

4. Find two consecutive odd integers such that three times the larger decreased by the smaller is 16.

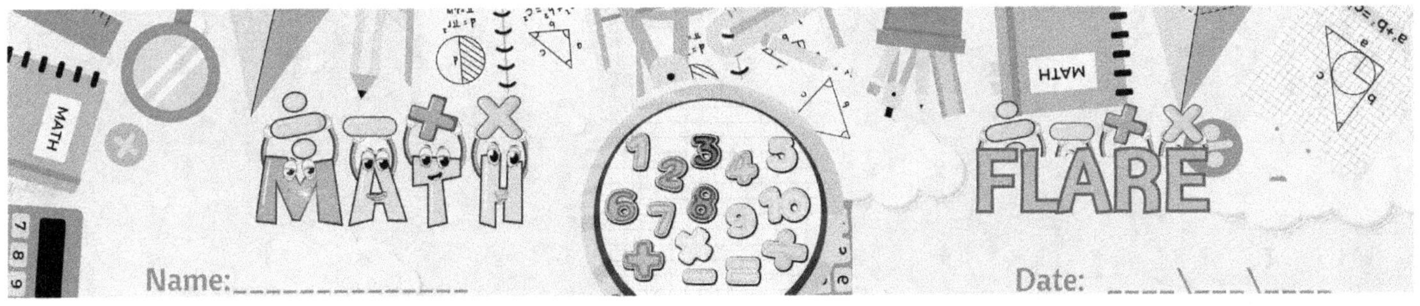

5. Seven more than four times a number is 15. What is the number?

6. The product of six and some number is equal to the sum of that number and 20. What is the number?

7. When a number is divided by nine, the result is 2. What is the number?

8. Four less than a number is 3. Find the number.

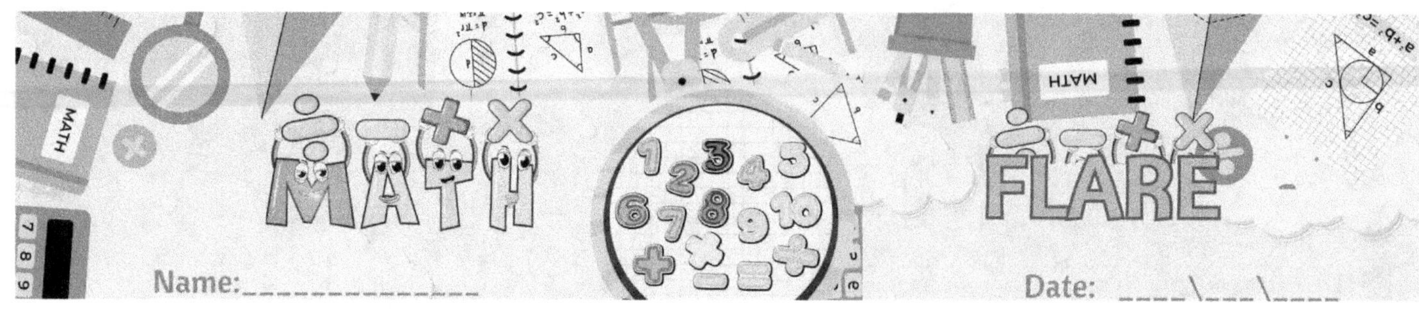

9. One number is 3 more than another number. The sum of twice the larger number and four times the smaller is 42. What are the numbers?

10. The sum of four consecutive even numbers is 44. What are the numbers?

11. Four times a number increased by 6 is 54. Find the number.

12. One number is nine more than another number. The sum of the larger number and twice the smaller number is 24. Find the numbers?

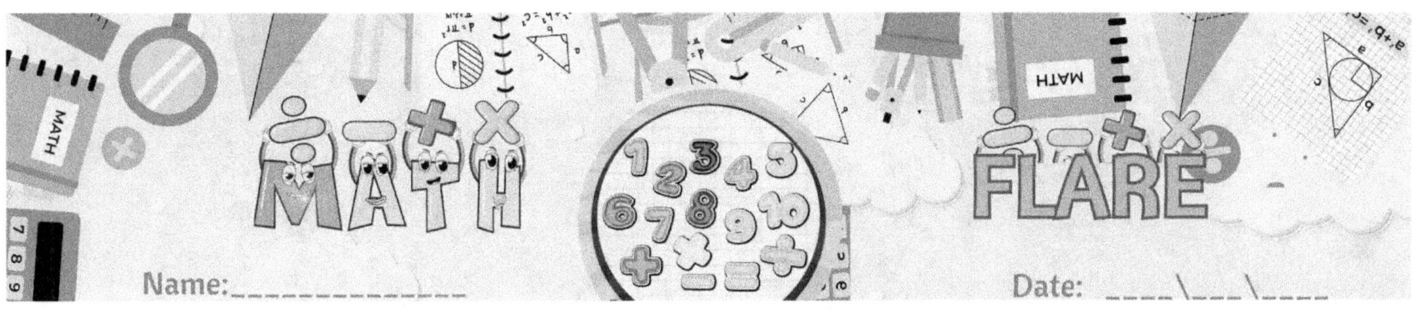

Name:_______________________   Date: _______________

13. The greater of two numbers is 10 less than nine times the smaller number. Their sum is 60. Find the numbers.

14. The sum of two numbers is 30. The larger number is four times the smaller number. What are the numbers?

15. One less than five times a number is 19. Find the number.

16. Eight less than a number is 3. Find the number.

17. The sum of the largest and six times the smallest of three consecutive numbers is equal to 23. Find the numbers.

18. The sum of a number and one is 4. Find the number.

19. One number is seven times another. Their sum is 56. Find the numbers.

20. The product of two numbers is 28. One number is three less than the other. What are the numbers?

21.   Six times the sum of a number and two times the number is 108. Find the number.

22.   One number is two times another. Their sum is 24. Find the numbers.

23.   If the product of eight and a number is increased by 5, the result is 77. Find the number?

24.   The sum of two numbers is 6. The larger number is two times the smaller number. What are the numbers?

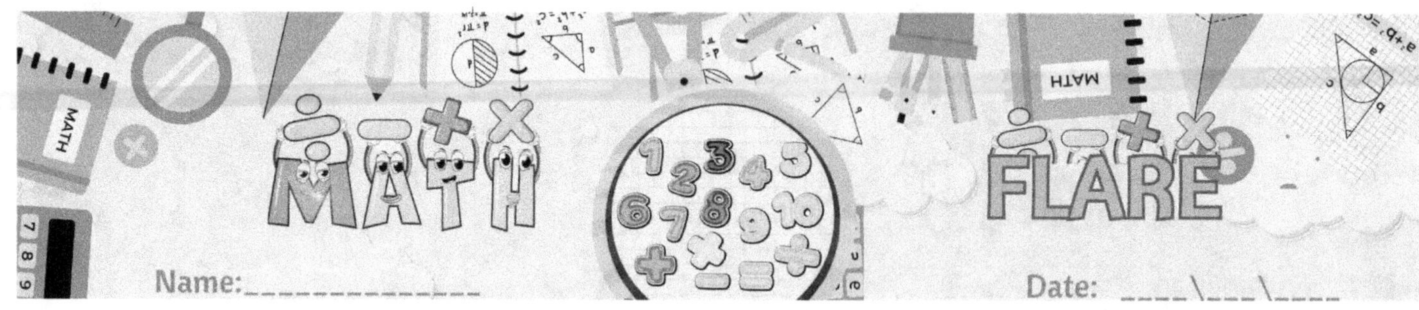

Name:________________   Date: ______________

25. The sum of three numbers is 62. The largest number is six times the smallest, and the smallest is six less than the middle number. Find the numbers.

26. The difference of two numbers is 15. The larger number is 3 more than seven times the smaller number. What are the numbers?

27. Nine more than five times a number is equal to the number increased by 29. What is the number?

28. Ten more than the second of three consecutive even integers is the same as the difference between the third and four times the first. Find the numbers.

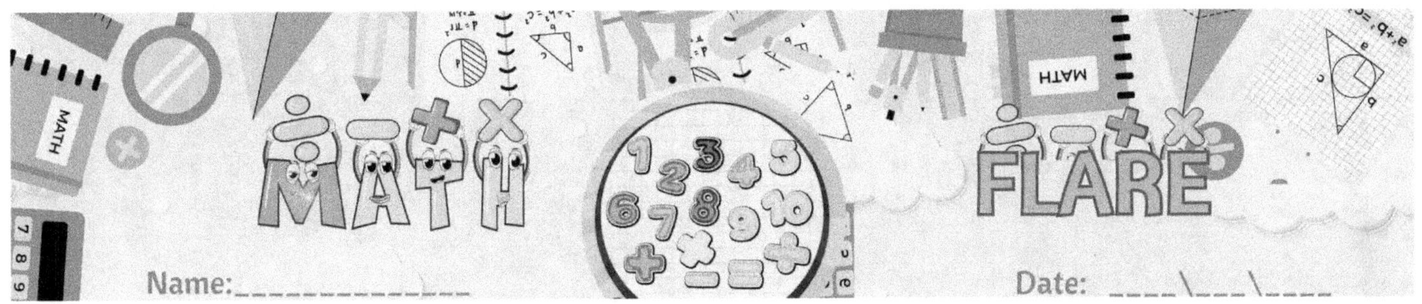

29. One of two numbers is ten more than the other. The sum of the numbers is 14. Find the numbers.

30. Find two consecutive odd integers such that three times the larger decreased by the smaller is 8.

31. Eight more than eight times a number is equal to the number increased by 71. What is the number?

32. One number is 4 more than another number. The sum of three times the larger number and five times the smaller is 44. What are the numbers?

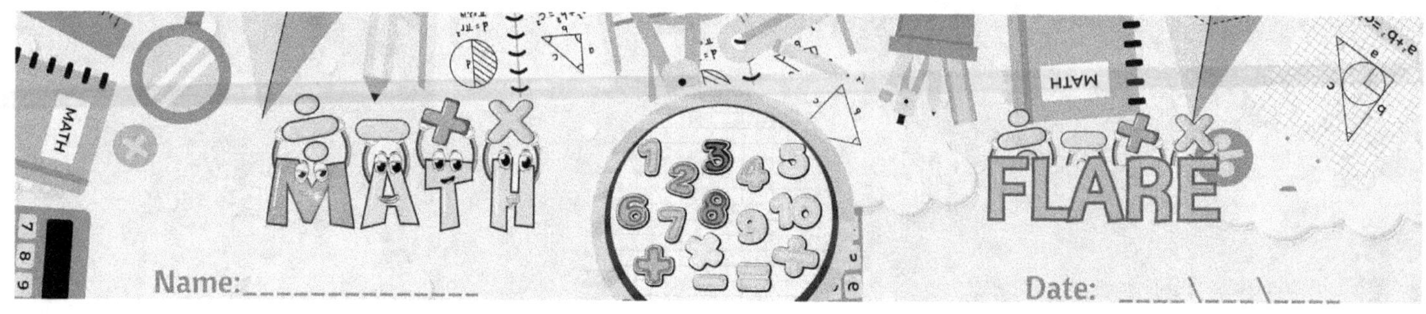

33. The sum of two numbers is 4. One number is two less than the other. Find the numbers.

34. Ten times the difference of 7 minus a number is 10. What is the number?

35. One of two numbers is ten more than the other. The sum of the numbers is 20. Find the numbers.

36. A number decreased by 3 is 1. Find the number.

37. Six more than five times a number is equal to the number increased by 54. What is the number?

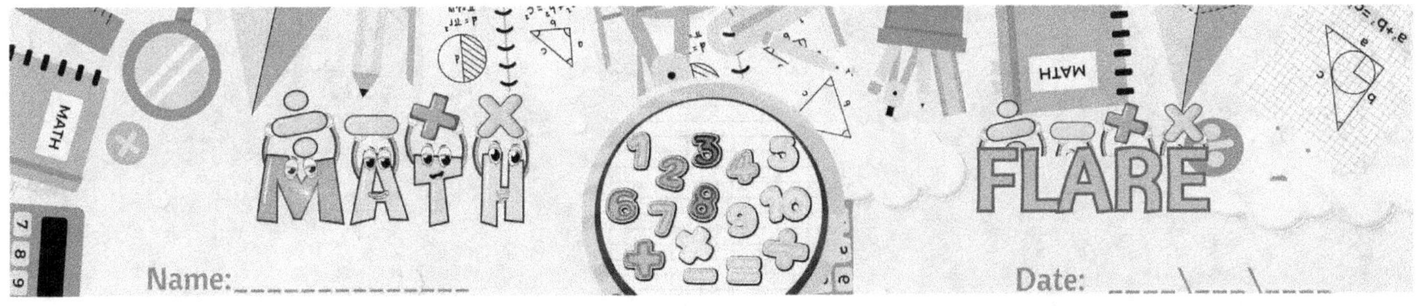

38.　Four times the sum of a number and three times the number is 144. Find the number.

39.　Five times a number equals 4 less than seven times the number. What is the number?

40.　Two-fifths of a number is 2. Find the number.

41.　Eight more than a number is 14. What is the number?

42.　Twice a number is 2. What is the number?

Graphing Linear Equations

1. 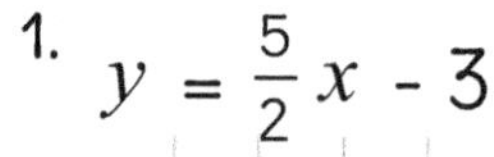
$$y = \frac{5}{2}x - 3$$

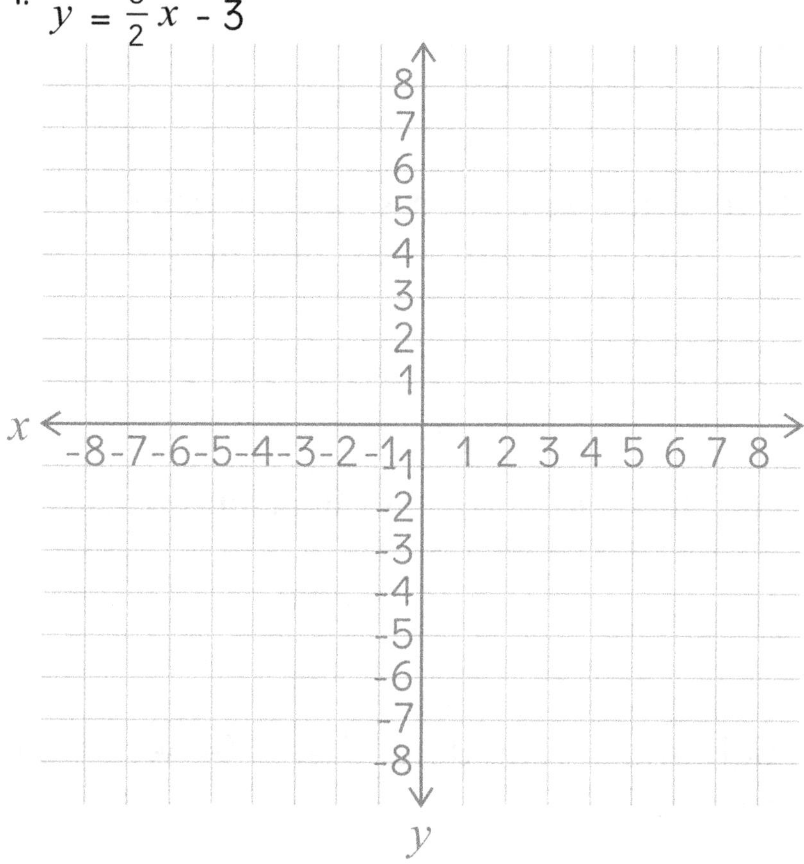

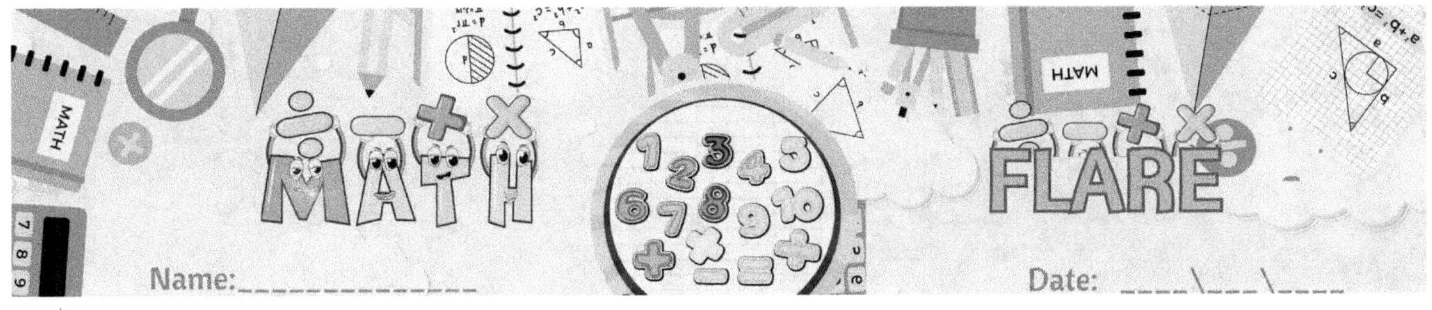

2. $y = + 3$

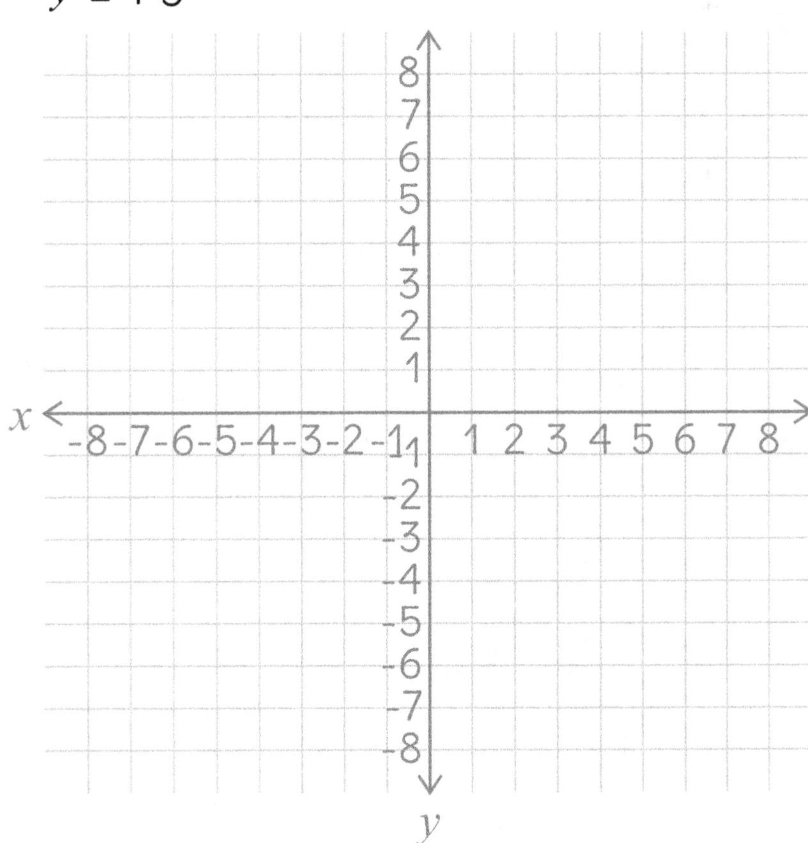

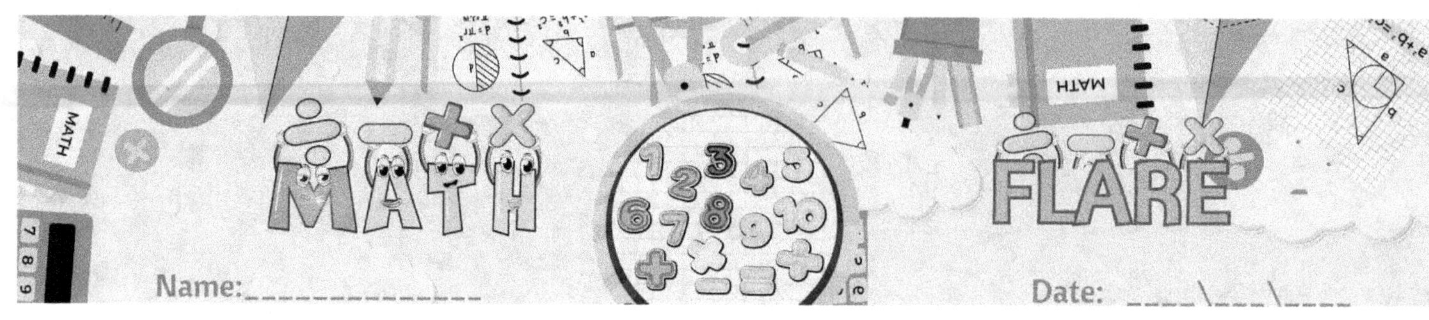

3.

$$y = \frac{-1}{2}x + 6$$

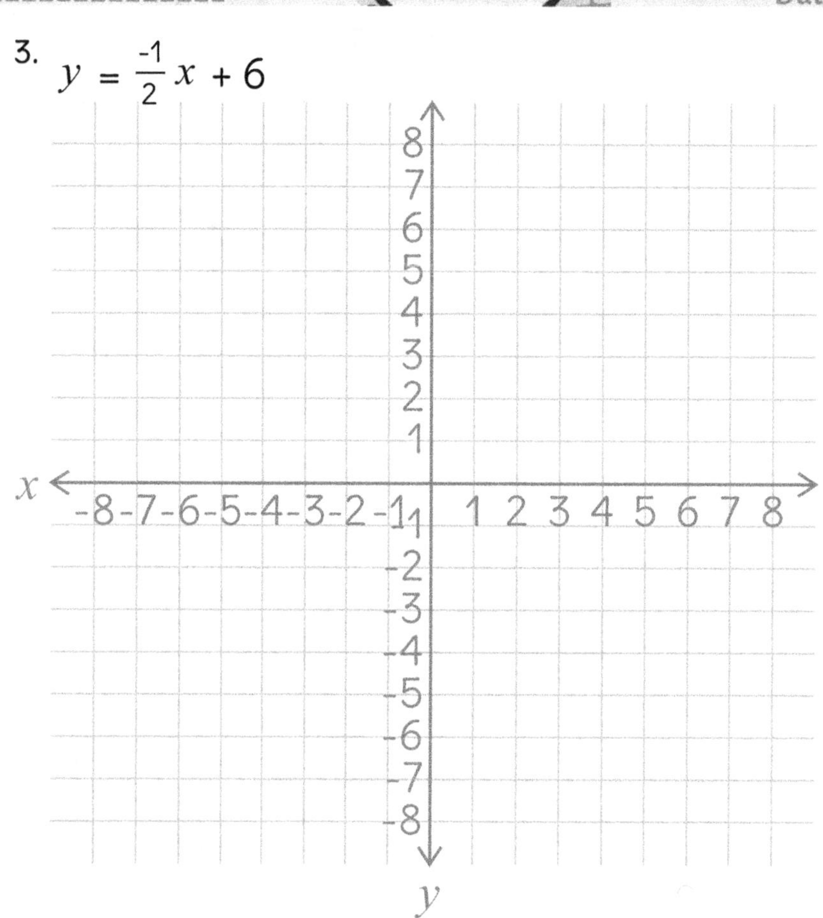

4. $y = \dfrac{-11}{4}x - 6$

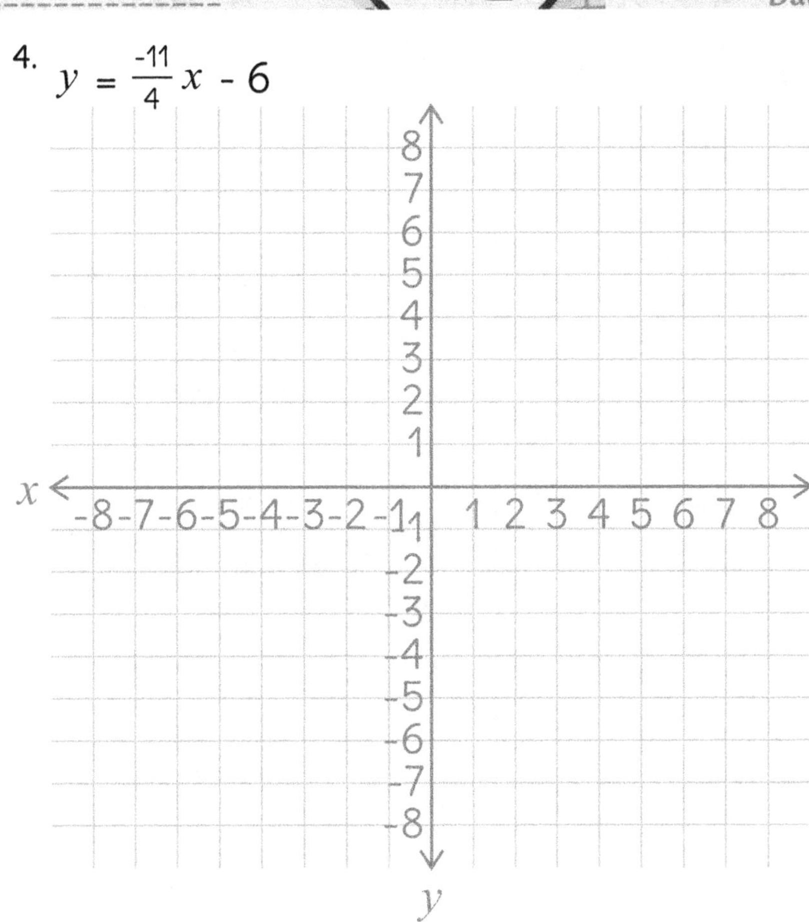

5.

$$y = 3x - 7$$

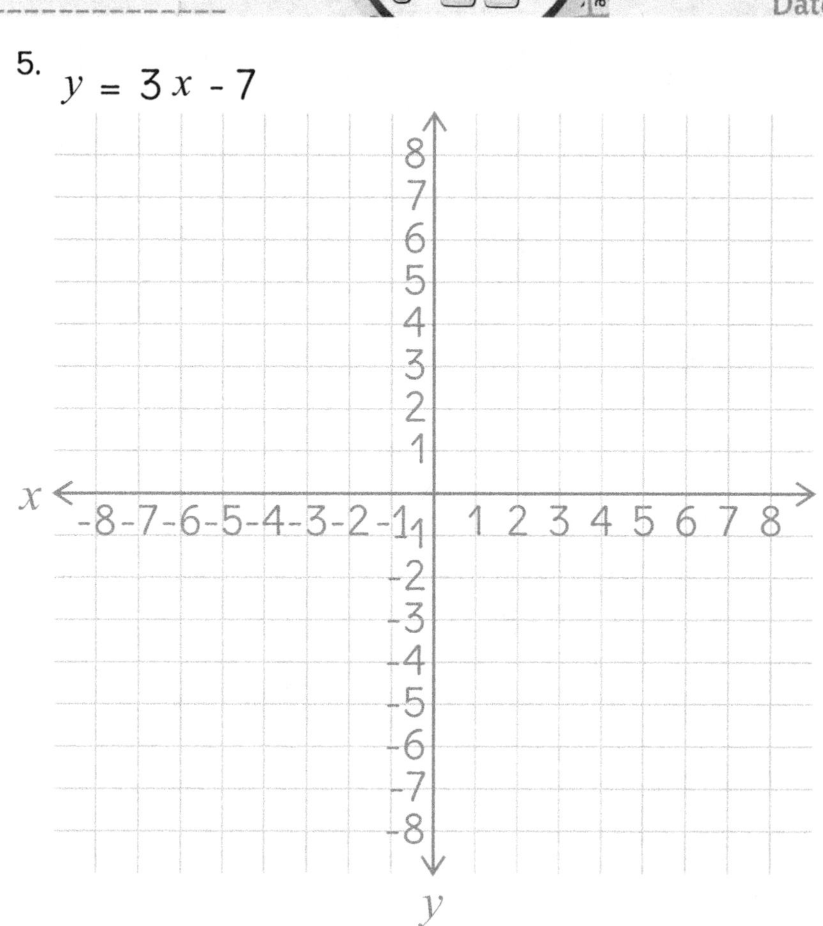

6. $y = +5$

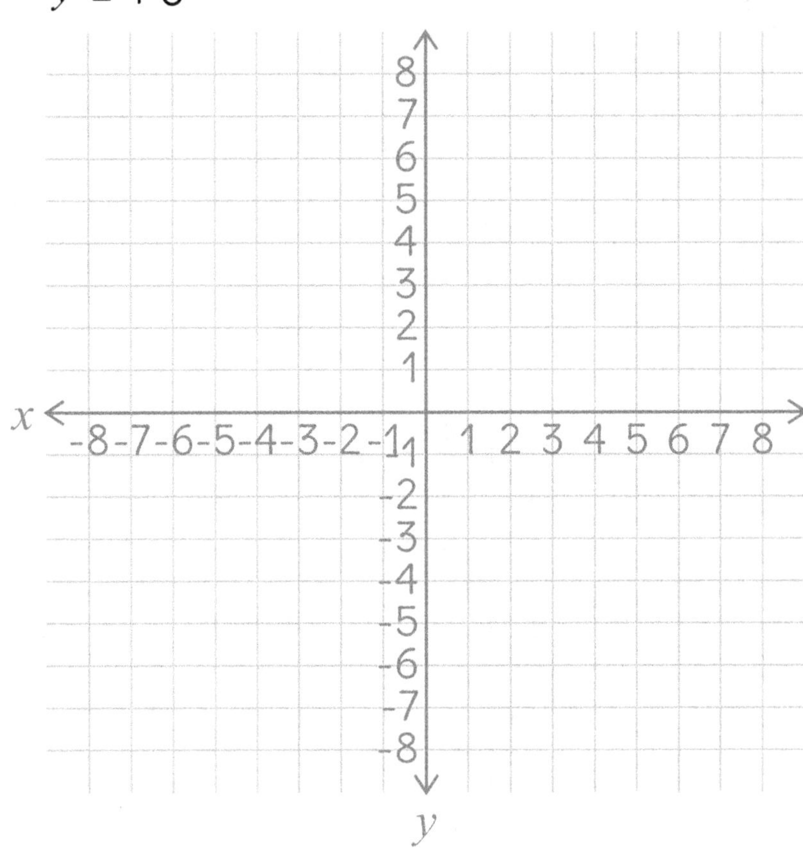

7. $y = \dfrac{9}{4}x - 1$

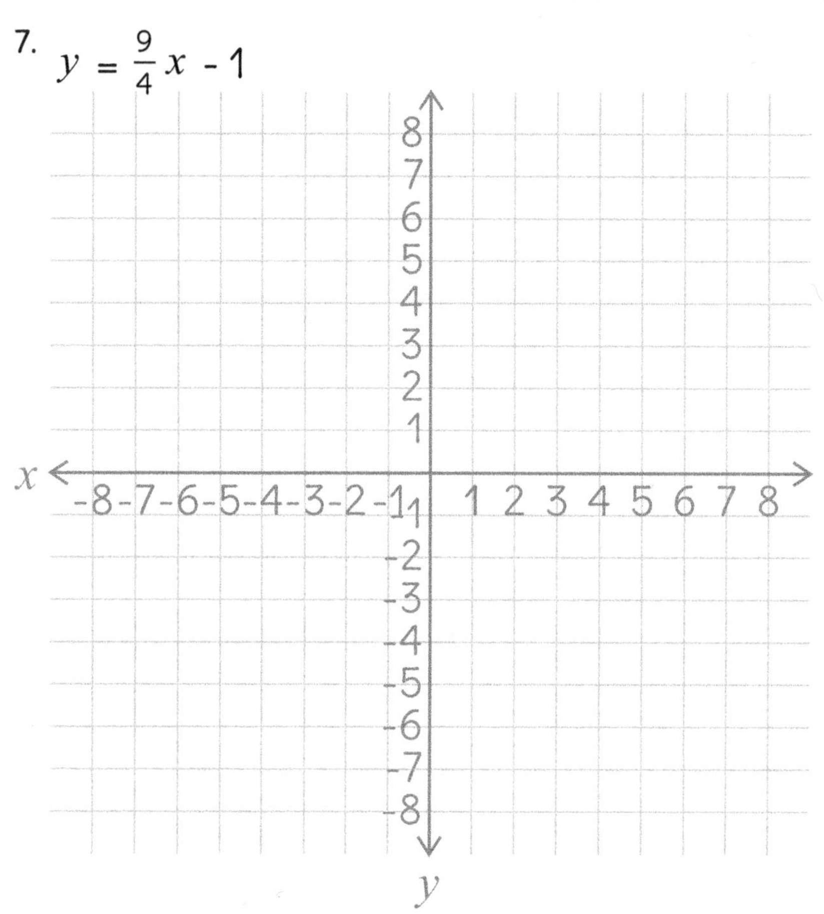

8. $y = \dfrac{-3}{4}x - 1$

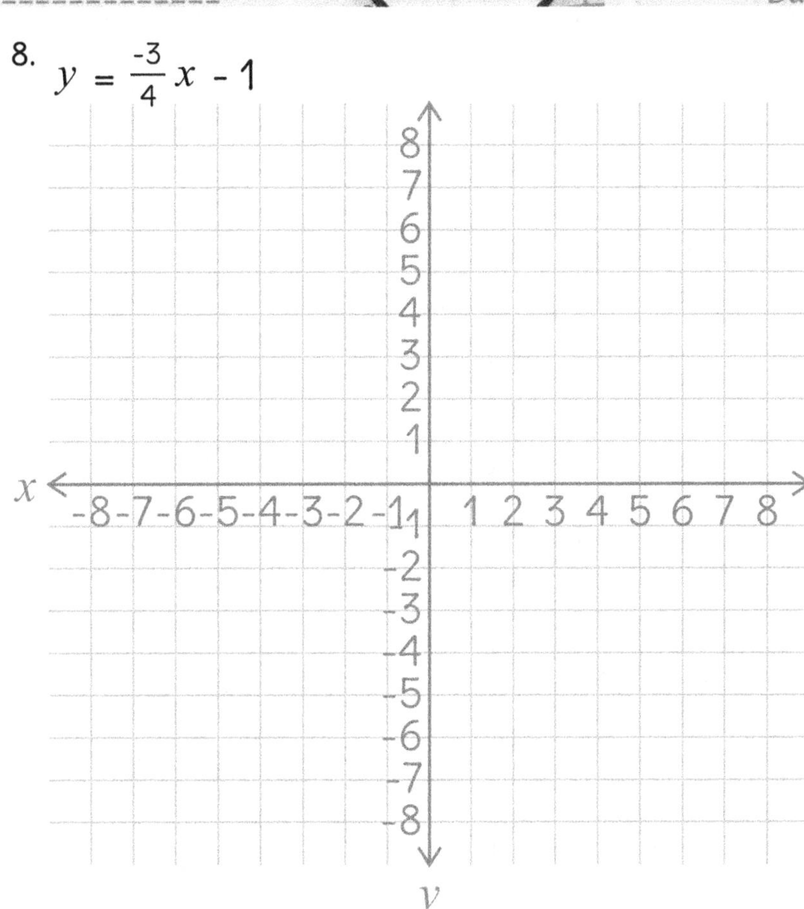

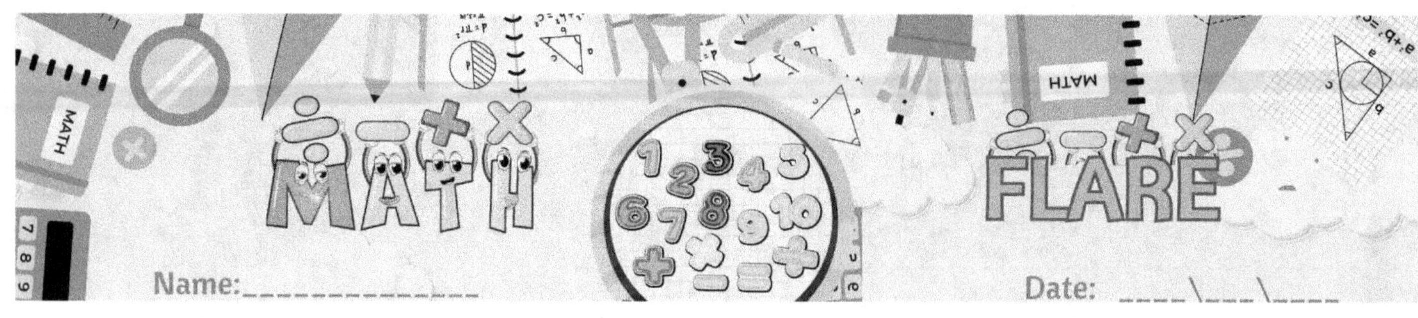

9. $y = \dfrac{-11}{4}x + 2$

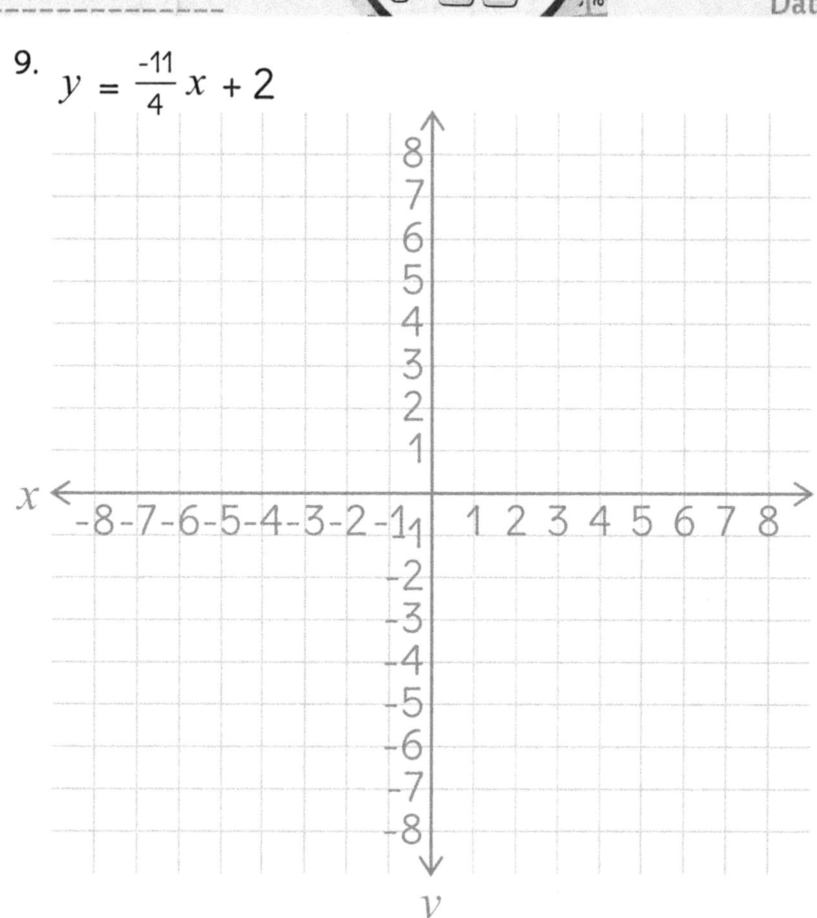

10. 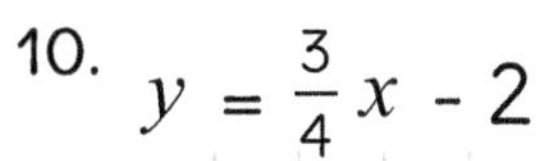 $y = \dfrac{3}{4}x - 2$

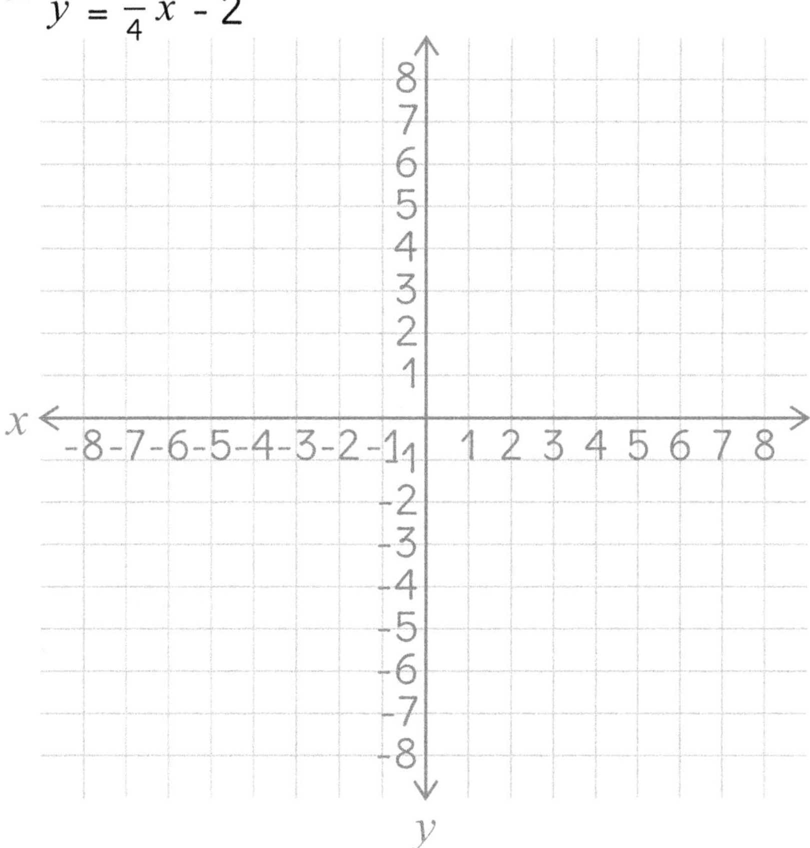

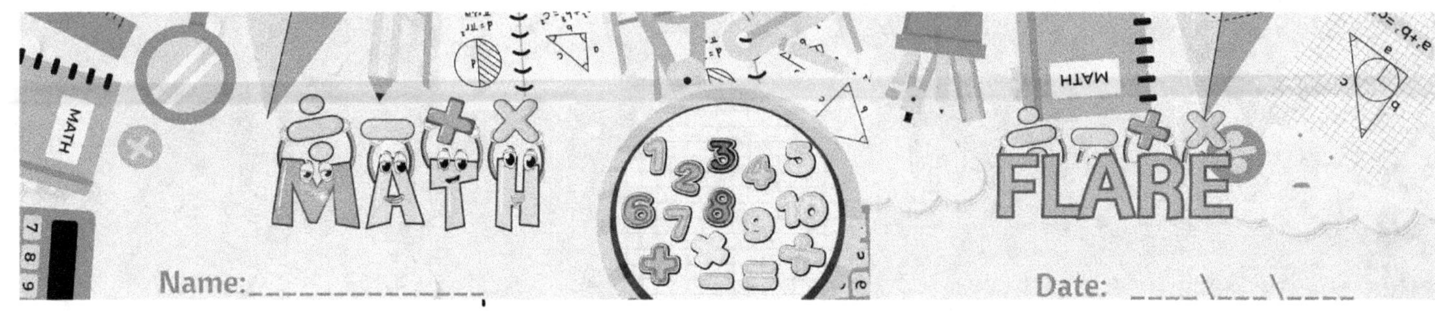

1. -6x + 6 = 42

2. 3x + 4 = 10

3. -2x + 9 = 29

4. 3x + 0 = 9

5. 10x + -9 = -59

6. 9x + -6 = -15

7. -7x + 2 = 51

8. -1x + -6 = 1

9. -1x + -2 = 0

10. 6x + 0 = -18

11. $-9x + 7 = 43$

12. $4x + -4 = -4$

13. $-4x + 10 = -2$

14. $7x + 2 = -19$

15. $4x + 4 = -36$

16. $10x + 8 = -2$

17. $-4x + 1 = -11$

18. $-6x + 5 = -55$

19. $-10x + 8 = -22$

20. $-5x + -5 = 25$

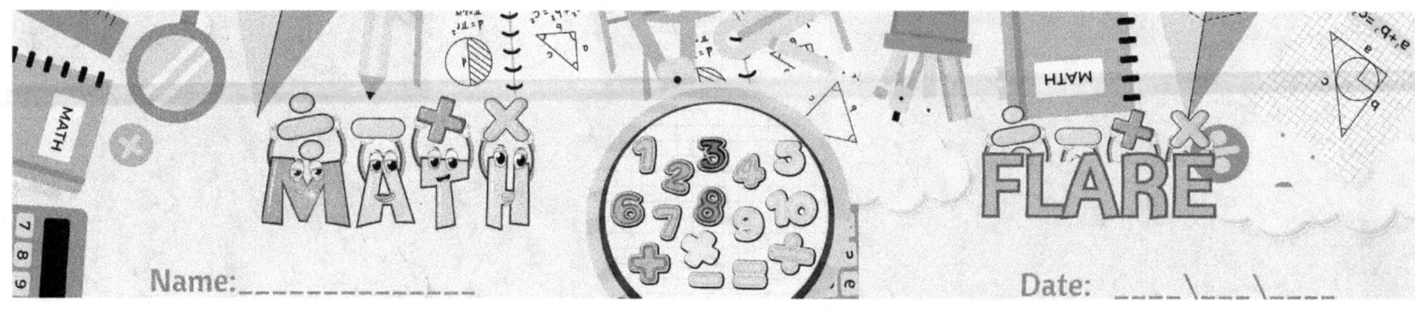

21. -10x + -3 = 27

22. -7x + 0 = -28

23. 4x + 5 = -23

24. 10x + -2 = 28

25. -10x + -9 = 81

26. 9x + -1 = 89

27. -3x + -7 = -19

28. 6x + -2 = 52

29. -5x + 1 = -49

30. -4x + -3 = -11

Find Slope from Two Points

1. - (10, 66) and (-6, -30)

2. (-7, -68) and (1, 12)

3. (9, 27) and (9, 27)

4. (4, -9) and (8, -21)

5. (-4, 7) and (-4, 7)

6. (-10, 66) and (-8, 54)

7. (-10, -70) and (-10, -70)

8. (-10, 77) and (-10, 77)

9. (6, 62) and (-3, -19)

10. (-7, -32) and (-2, -2)

11. (-6, 5) and (-8, 9)

16. (-4, -9) and (5, 0)

12. (2, -6) and (7, -16)

17. (3, 33) and (-4, -23)

13. (-8, 48) and (-8, 48)

18. (8, -28) and (0, 4)

14. (-1, -16) and (-6, -56)

19. (0, 2) and (-9, -7)

15. (-9, -51) and (-6, -33)

20. (3, -16) and (5, -28)

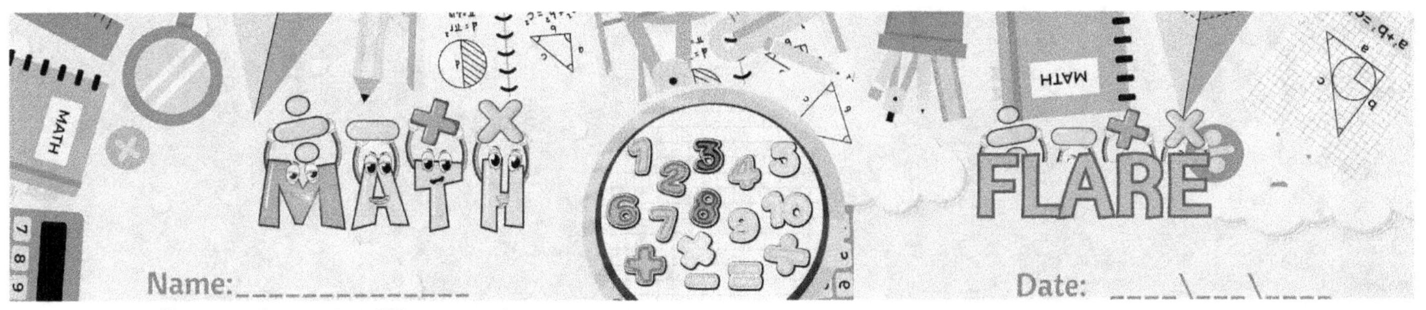

Quadratic Equations

1. $-3x^2 + 11x - 2 = 0$

2. $6n^2 - 24 = 0$

3. $-2v^2 + 24 = 0$

4. $-x^2 + 12x - 7 = 0$

5. $-p^2 - 2p + 120 = 0$

6. $6a^2 + 8a - 128 = 0$

7. $6k^2 + 9k - 132 = 0$

8. $6x^2 - 96 = 0$

9. $5r^2 - 8r - 17 = 0$

10. $3n^2 - 108 = 0$

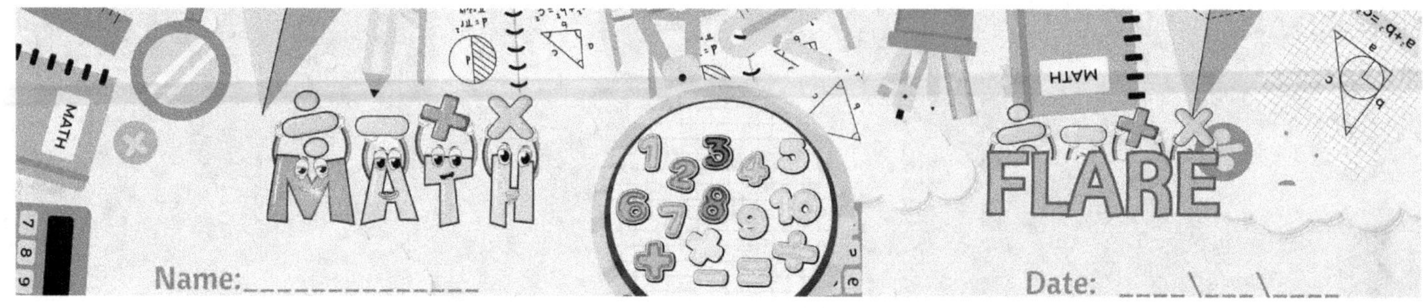

11. $6a^2 - 14 = 5$

16. $-n^2 - 8n + 73 = -11$

12. $-5b^2 + 12b + 20 = 2$

17. $4x^2 - 9x = 9$

13. $-4r^2 - 12r + 3 = -4$

18. $-6v^2 - 2v + 109 = 5$

14. $9b^2 + 7b - 3 = 6$

19. $-9p^2 - 10 = -9$

15. $4p^2 - 4p - 25 = 10$

20. $-5n^2 + 4n + 66 = 9$

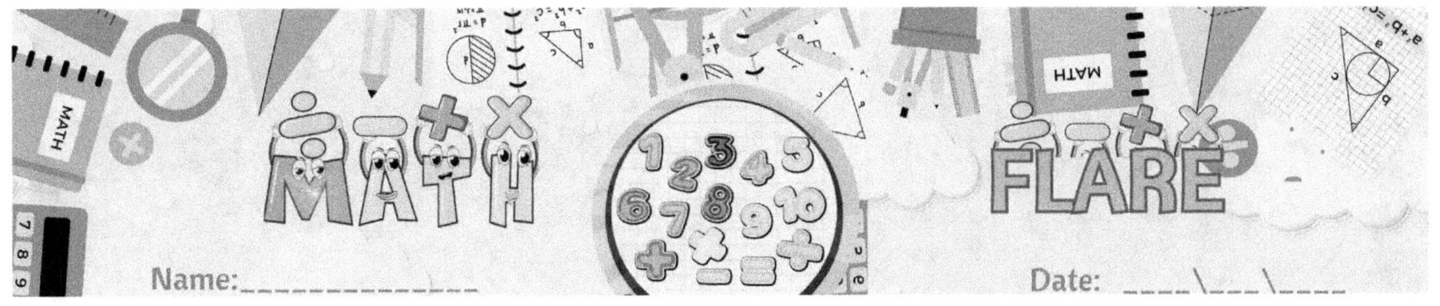

21. $7b^2 + 7 = -7b$

22. $-11x^2 - 12x = -21$

23. $9k^2 = 2k + 21$

24. $-6x^2 = 2x - 8$

25. $6x^2 - 10x = 24$

26. $4a^2 - 81 = 0$

27. $5k^2 - 8 = -3k$

28. $-11v^2 + 3v = -7$

29. $-10n^2 = 8 + 6n$

30. $9v^2 - 22 = 12v$

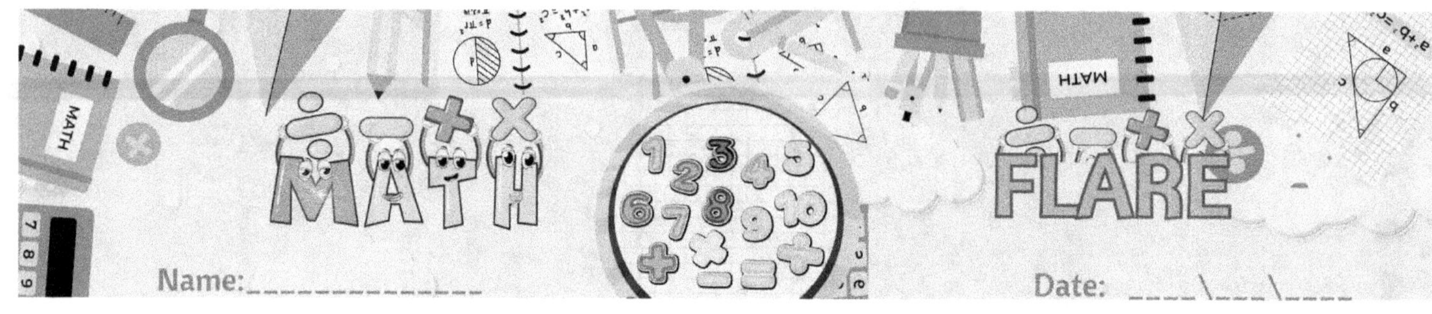

31. $9x^2 = 23$

32. $-7r^2 + 6r = -9$

33. $-3x^2 = 5x - 23$

34. $b^2 - 121 = 0$

35. $10\,p^2 = 4$

36. $2r^2 + 7r = 99$

37. $-4n^2 = -36$

38. $5k^2 = 18 - k$

39. $11n^2 - 10n = 3$

40. $5x^2 - x = 84$

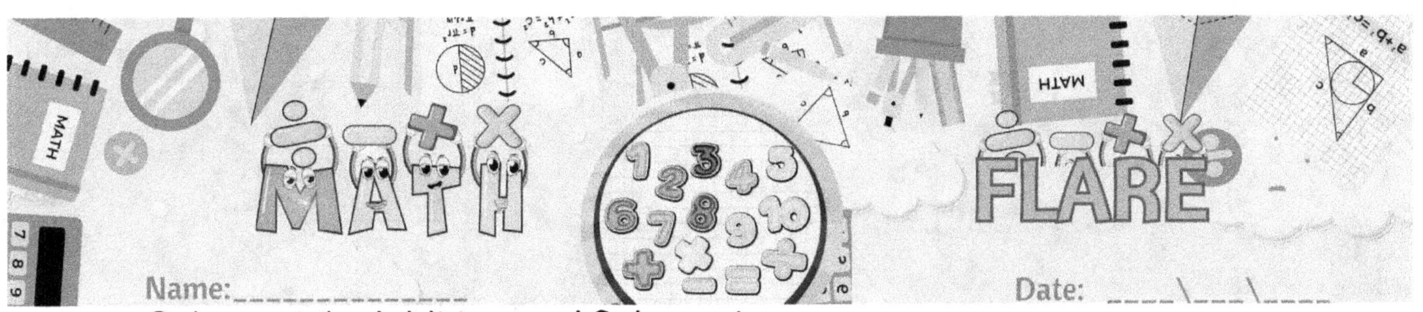

Polynomials: Addition and Subtraction

1. $(7n^3 + 7n^2) + (5n^3 + 7n^2)$

2. $(4x + 7) + (4 + x)$

3. $(k^2 - k^4) - (5k^3 - k^4)$

4. $(r^2 - 3r) - (5r - 7r^2)$

5. $(5r^3 - 6r^4) - (6r^4 - 7r^3)$

6. $(r^3 + 8) + (5r + 2r^3)$

7. $(5x + 1) - (3 - 5x)$

8. $(m^4 - 2) - (2m + 4)$

9. $(7 - 3n) - (7 + 2n)$

10. $(3n + n^4) - (2n + 4n^4)$

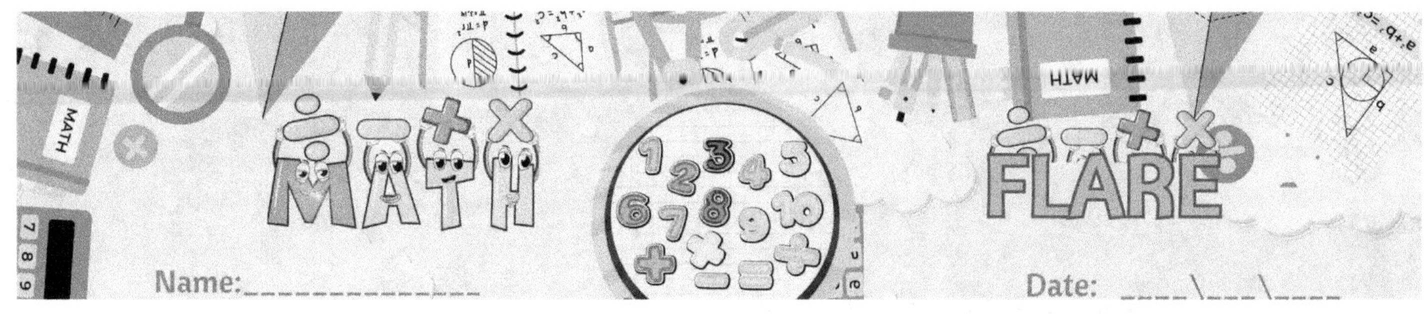

11. $(8x^3 - 2) - (8x^4 + 7x^3 - 6)$

16. $(8 - 6n^3) - (7n^4 + 7n^3 + 4)$

12. $(8a^4 + 7a^3) - (8a^3 + 8a + a^4)$

17. $(2x^4 + 1) + (3 - 2x^4 - 7x)$

13. $(5p^3 + 3) - (4 + p^2 + 6p^3)$

18. $(8 - 2r) - (7r + 8 + 5r^2)$

14. $(2x^4 + 2x^3) - (x^4 - 2 - x^3)$

19. $(2n^2 + 5n^3) + (8n^4 - 8n^2 + 7n^3)$

15. $(1 + 4v^2) + (3v^2 - v + 6)$

20. $(2k^3 + 4k) + (2k^4 - 5k + k^3)$

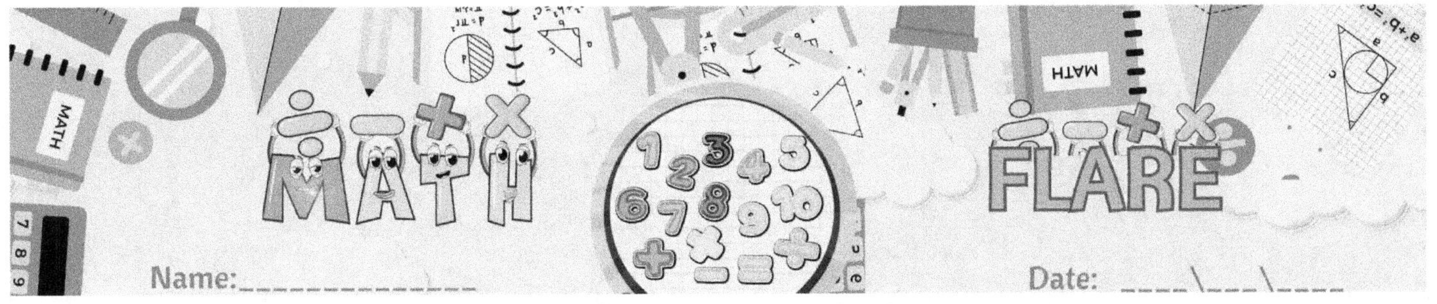

21. $(5 - 2x + 2x^4) + (4 + 4x - 5x^2)$

22. $(2n^3 + 4n + n^4) - (8n^4 + 6n^3 - 3n)$

23. $(3 + 6r^4 - 5r^2) - (4r^2 + 1 + 2r^4)$

24. $(3n - 5n^4 - 7) + (2n + 4n^2 - 5)$

25. $(7 + 2x - 6x^4) - (6x - 7 + 8x^4)$

26. $(3v^4 + 7v - 6) + (6 - 7v^4 + 5v)$

27. $(6x - 1 + 5x^3) - (3x^3 - 3x^4 - 8)$

28. $(8r^3 + 6r - 7) - (r^4 + 4r^3 - 2)$

29. $(8r^3 + 5r + 7r^2) - (5r^3 - 8r^2 + 7r)$

30. $(8x^4 + 8x - 4) + (7x^4 + 3x - 8)$

ANSWERS

Page 1:   Solving Two-Step Equations

1. 9	2. 4	3. 1	4. 1	5. 8	6. 6	7. 3	8. 10	9. 10
10. 4	11. 2	12. 1	13. 3	14. 8	15. 8	16. 2	17. 2	18. 6
19. 8	20. 6	21. 8	22. 9	23. 9	24. 8	25. 10	26. 8	27. 8
28. 4	29. 9	30. 3	31. 8	32. 9	33. 8	34. 10	35. 1	36. 6
37. 8	38. 1	39. 6	40. 8	41. 9	42. 10	43. 4	44. 10	45. 9
46. 4	47. 9	48. 4						

Page 7:   Solving Multi-Step Equations

1. 10	2. 6
3. 5	4. 8
5. 4	6. 2
7. 3	8. 5
9. 9	10. 1
11. 5	12. 6
13. 7	14. 10
15. 3 or -199 or -198 or -197 or...	16. 2 or -199 or -198 or -197 or...
17. 8	18. 6
19. 6	20. 3
21. 1	22. 10
23. 6	24. 2

25. 3	26. 2
27. 9	28. 6
29. 10	30. 1
31. 3	32. 2
33. 1	34. 8
35. 1	36. 4
37. 7	38. 10
39. 6	40. 3
41. 5	42. 3
43. 10	44. 7
45. 4	46. 6
47. 5	48. 5
49. 10	50. 10
51. 1	52. 9
53. 3	54. 6
55. 1	56. 10

Page 14: Equations (Two Sides)

1. $x = -9$ 2. $x = -3$ 3. $m = 6$ 4. $z = -7$ 5. $z = -2$

6. $a = 5$ 7. $b = -7$ 8. $b = -5$ 9. $k = 1$ 10. $k = 3$

11. $a = 5$ 12. $b = 4$ 13. $b = 3$ 14. $a = 1$ 15. $a = -8$

16. $z = -4$ 17. $y = -1$ 18. $z = 7$ 19. $x = -10$ 20. $z = 8$

21. s = 4   22. m = -2   23. z = -5   24. k = 1   25. y = -6

26. s = -7   27. z = 6   28. a = 10   29. x = 5   30. z = -6

31. y = 9   32. s = -4   33. k = 2   34. y = 9   35. s = -2

36. z = -4   37. z = 4   38. z = 6   39. k = -1   40. a = 5

41. z = 8   42. s = -4   43. a = 5   44. x = -9   45. y = -1

46. x = -2   47. z = 7   48. b = 1   49. m = -10   50. m = 3

51. b = -10   52. s = -10   53. y = -6   54. b = -8   55. x = -8

56. b = -2

Page 21: Simplify Expressions

1. $-11y - 10$ 2. $-4z + 15$ 3. $-16m + 11$ 4. $3z$

5. $-18m + 29$ 6. $24z + 3$ 7. $-14y + 11$ 8. $-12k$

9. $-18y - 13$ 10. $-14z + 7$ 11. $3k + 4$ 12. $10y + 18$

13. $15k - 12$ 14. $10k + 10$ 15. $16z$ 16. $85z - 213$

17. $-8x - 3$ 18. $-18m - 11$ 19. $30y + 35$ 20. $176k - 301$

21. $-26y + 16$ 22. $-18x + 47$ 23. $-8m + 14$ 24. $3m + 3$

25. $-4z + 3$ 26. 2 27. $24y - 13$ 28. $198k + 31$

29. $-2m + 3$ 30. $8m + 13$ 31. $30z + 40$ 32. $-11y + 1$

33. $37k + 1$ 34. $-22y + 3$ 35. $18k + 5$ 36. $9k + 4$

37. $-28y - 6$ 38. $5m + 9$ 39. $-18k$ 40. $-17z + 2$

41. -17 42. $25z + 3$ 43. $-y$ 44. $-37k - 20$

45. $-24x + 21$ 46. $19m + 15$ 47. $-15k$ 48. $-39z + 37$

49. 30k + 28   50. 16z   51. -8x + 33   52. 285m - 110

53. -27m - 6   54. 23y   55. -17k + 1   56. 29m + 2

Page 28: Evaluating Equations
1. 97   2. 34   3. 24   4. 12   5. -2   6. 32   7. -23   8. -8

Page 29: Evaluating Equations
1. -144   2. -8   3. 4   4. -12   5. -16   6. 132   7. -70   8. -16

Page 30: Evaluating Equations
1. 143   2. -729   3. -10   4. -12   5. 0   6. 20   7. -747

8. -599

Page 31: Evaluating Equations
1. 66   2. 12   3. -660   4. 82   5. 97   6. 103   7. -36

8. 66

Page 32: Evaluating Equations
1. -4   2. -37   3. 32   4. 8   5. -18   6. 22   7. -4   8. -13

Page 33: Evaluating Equations
1. -35   2. -51   3. 8   4. 4   5. -15   6. 7   7. -45   8. 41

Page 34: Evaluating Equations
1. -59   2. 2,401   3. -10   4. -0.6   5. 0   6. -210   7. 53

8. -9.1

Page 35: Verbal Algebra Expressions
1. 1   2. 8, 2   3. 4, 24   4. 5, 7

5. 2   6. 4   7. 18   8. 7

9. 6, 9   10. 8, 10, 12, 14   11. 12   12. 14, 5

13. 53, 7   14. 6, 24   15. 4   16. 11

17. 3, 4, 5   18. 3   19. 7, 49   20. 7, 4

21. 6   22. 8, 16   23. 9   24. 2, 4

25. 7, 13, 42   26. 2, 17   27. 5   28. 8, 10, 12

29. 2, 12   30. 1, 3   31. 9   32. 4, 8

33. 3, 1   34. 6   35. 5, 15   36. 4

37. 12   38. 9   39. 2   40. 5

41. 6   42. 1

Page 45: Graphing Linear Equations

1. $y = \frac{5}{2}x - 3$

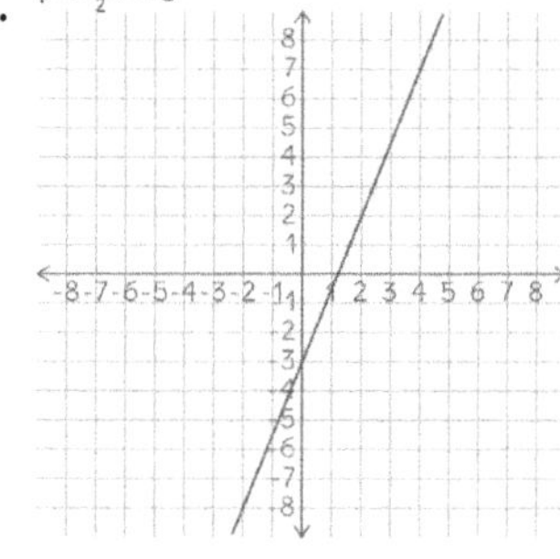

2. $y = + 3$

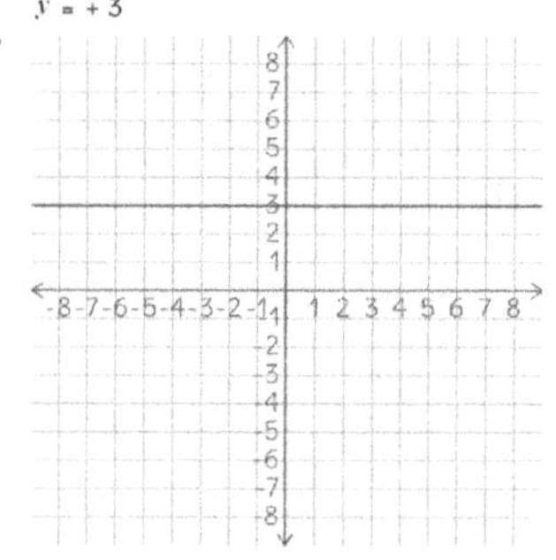

3. $y = \frac{-1}{2}x + 6$

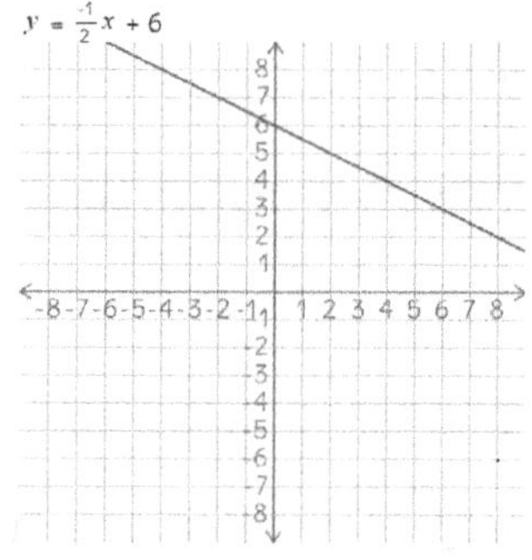

4. $y = \frac{-11}{4}x - 6$

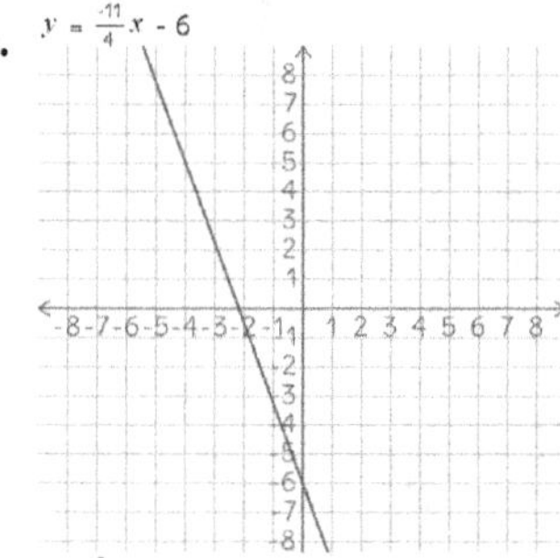

5. $y = 3x - 7$

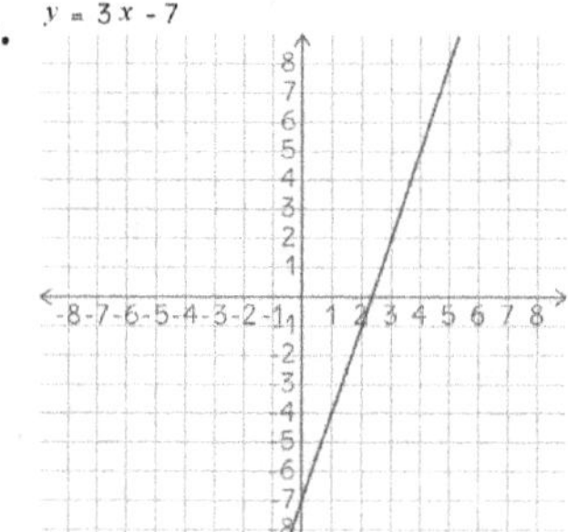

6. $y = + 5$

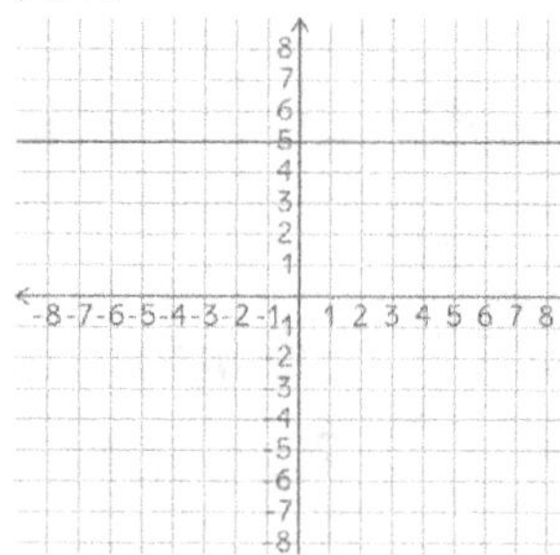

7. $y = \frac{9}{4}x - 1$

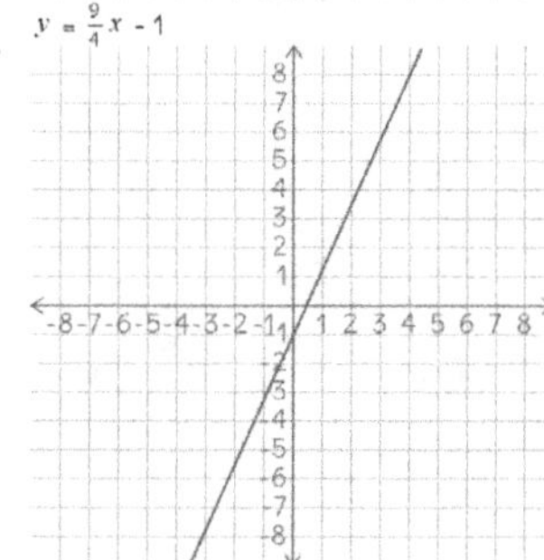

8. $y = \frac{-3}{4}x - 1$

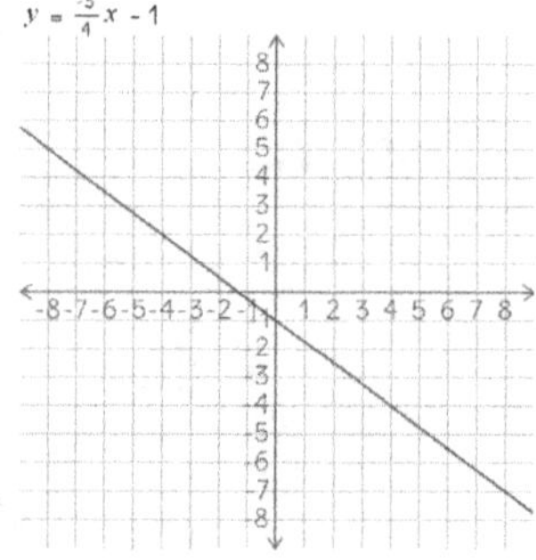

9. $y = \frac{-11}{4}x + 2$

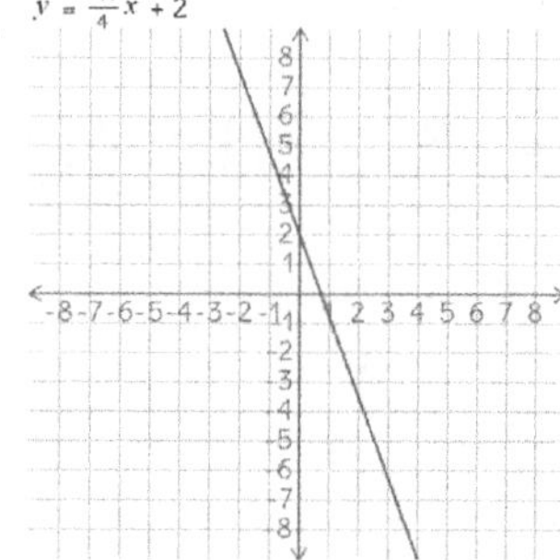

10. 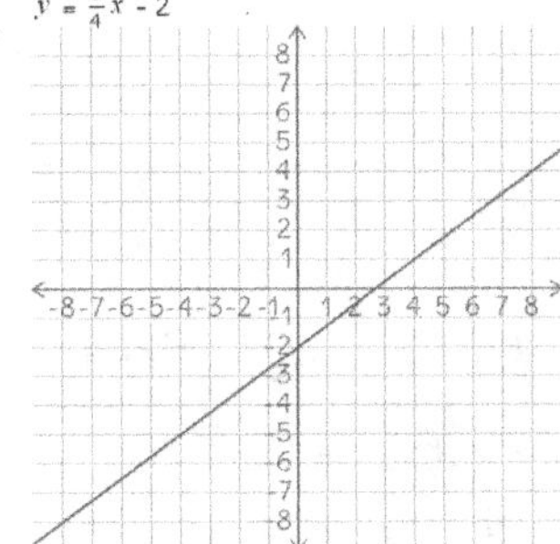

$y = \frac{3}{4}x - 2$

Page 55: Standard Linear Equations

1. -6
2. 2
3. -10
4. 3
5. -5
6. -1
7. -7
8. -7
9. -2
10. -3

11. -4
12. 0
13. 3
14. -3
15. -10
16. -1
17. 3
18. 10
19. 3
20. -6

21. -3
22. 4
23. -7
24. 3
25. -9
26. 10
27. 4
28. 9
29. 10
30. 2

Page 58: Find Slope from Two Points

1. 6
2. 10
3. 4
4. -3
5. -1
6. -6
7. 7

8. -7
9. 9
10. 6
11. -2
12. -2
13. -6
14. 8

15. 6
16. 1
17. 8
18. -4
19. 1
20. -6

Page 60: Quadratic Equations

1. (0.192, 3.475)
2. (2, -2)
3. (-3.464, 3.464)
4. (0.615, 11.385)
5. (-12, 10)
6. (4, -5.333)
7. (4, -5.5)
8. (4, -4)
9. (2.81, -1.21)
10. (6, -6)
11. (1.78, -1.78)
12. (-1.045, 3.445)
13. (-3.5, 0.5)
14. (0.684, -1.462)
15. (3.5, -2.5)
16. (-14, 6)
17. (3, -0.75)
18. (-4.333, 4)
19. No real solution.
20. (-3, 3.8)
21. No real solution.
22. (-2.031, 0.94)
23. (1.643, -1.42)
24. (-1.333, 1)
25. (3, -1.333)
26. (4.5, -4.5)
27. (1, -1.6)
28. (-0.673, 0.946)
29. No real solution.
30. (2.366, -1.033)
31. (1.599, -1.599)
32. (-0.784, 1.641)
33. (-3.725, 2.058)
34. (11, -11)
35. (0.632, -0.632)
36. (5.5, -9)
37. (-3, 3)
38. (1.8, -2)
39. (1.147, -0.238)
40. (4.2, -4)

Page 64: Polynomials: Addition and Subtraction

1. $12n^3 + 14n^2$
2. $5x + 11$
3. $-5k^3 + k^2$
4. $8r^2 - 8r$
5. $-12r^4 + 12r^3$
6. $3r^3 + 5r + 8$
7. $10x - 2$
8. $m^4 - 2m - 6$
9. $-5n$
10. $-3n^4 + n$
11. $-8x^4 + x^3 + 4$
12. $7a^4 - a^3 - 8a$
13. $- p^3 - p^2 - 1$
14. $x^4 + 3x^3 + 2$
15. $7v^2 - v + 7$
16. $-7n^4 - 13n^3 + 4$
17. $-7x + 4$
18. $-5r^2 - 9r$
19. $8n^4 + 12n^3 - 6n^2$
20. $2k^4 + 3k^3 - k$
21. $2x^4 - 5x^2 + 2x + 9$
22. $-7n^4 - 4n^3 + 7n$
23. $4r^4 - 9r^2 + 2$
24. $-5n^4 + 4n^2 + 5n - 12$
25. $-14x^4 - 4x + 14$
26. $-4v^4 + 12v$
27. $3x^4 + 2x^3 + 6x + 7$
28. $-r^4 + 4r^3 + 6r - 5$
29. $3r^3 + 15r^2 - 2r$
30. $15x^4 + 11x - 12$

www.ingramcontent.com/pod-product-compliance
Lightning Source LLC
Chambersburg PA
CBHW080741180726
48003CB00023B/3236